By Damon Veach

Information about the German families who settled in this area of Louisiana is available at Loyola University.

Dr. Ellen C. Merrill of The Historic New Orleans Collection, says that Special Collections at Loyola University has an uncatalogued group of papers given to the archive by the widow of J. Hanno Deiler, author of "Settlement of the German Coast and the Creoles of German Descent."

The collection contains work done by Deiler when compiling the genealogical section of the book. There are about 30 intricate genealogies of the original German families who settled in this area, many of whom have a vast number of descendants in the area today.

Long typed scripts (sometimes five to six pages, single-spaced) exist for the following families: Hymel, Tegre, Chantze, Mayer, Zeringue, Hertle, Wichner, Friedrich, Wiltz, Helte, Foltz, Leche, D'Arensburg, Krebs, Kleinpeter, Ory, Cambre, Huber, Kerne, Trische, Troxler and Zweig. Much harder to read are the hand-written genealogies of the Hofmann, Jacob, Ettler, Percle, Element, Edelmayer, Rixner, Bura and Schexschnaider families.

Mark Flynn, chief archivist of Loyola's Special Collections, says he will be happy to give permission for use of the material, and photocopies are also available.

Any further information should be directed to Dr. Merrill, The Historic New Orleans Collection, 533 Royal St., New Orleans, La. 70130.

(Note: The Historic New Orleans Collection offers researchers one of the finest facilities in the state. Don't overlook this when doing genealogical work in New Orleans.)

The Times-Picayune   Sunday, November 14, 1982

The Settlement of the German
Coast of Louisiana

D'ARENSBOURG

From a photograph taken by Miss Betsy Swanson, Department of Art, Newcomb College, Tulane University of a portrait in the collection of Mr. Felix H. Kuntz, New Orleans, Louisiana.

The Settlement of the German
Coast of Louisiana

AND

The Creoles of German Descent

BY J. HANNO DEILER

With a New

Preface, Chronology and Index

by

Jack Belsom

GENEALOGICAL PUBLISHING CO., INC.
BALTIMORE   1975

Originally Published
Philadelphia, 1909

Americana Germanica
New Series, Number 8

Reprinted with added Preface, Chronology,
Index, Frontispiece, and Half-Title
Genealogical Publishing Co., Inc.
Baltimore, 1969
Baltimore, 1970
Baltimore, 1975

Library of Congress Catalogue Card Number 67-28597
International Standard Book Number 0-8063-0092-2

PREFACE

J. Hanno Deiler was born August 8, 1849, at Altoetting in Upper Bavaria in the German empire, the second son of Konrad Deiler, a royal court musician and a descendant of an ancient family of Nuremberg. He was educated in the public schools and, in addition, received musical training from his father. At the age of ten he became choir soloist at the church of St. Emmeran at Ratisbon (Regensburg). In 1868 he graduated from the Royal Normal College of Munich and taught in several schools in Germany. Then, in January 1872, he emigrated to the United States and settled in New Orleans where he had been engaged as principal of a German school. In 1879 he was appointed professor of German in the University of Louisiana, now Tulane University. He was involved in many aspects of German culture, history, and music in New Orleans and was organizer and conductor of the 26th National Saengerfest in New Orleans in February 1890. His published works include, in addition to this volume, a number of books and articles relating to the Germans in New Orleans and the South. Professor Deiler died at his home in Covington, Louisiana on July 20, 1909.

For over half a century, J. Hanno Deiler's The Settlement of the German Coast of Louisiana and the Creoles of German Descent has been a valuable reference for historians and genealogists who sought a wider knowledge of the earliest German and Swiss settlers in Louisiana and particularly in that area along the Mississippi River west of New Orleans known as Des Allemands — The German coast.

And yet, as even the casual student will soon discover, Deiler's book is at once rewarding and frustrating, yielding priceless bits of information but also marred by some serious errors, poorly organized chronologically, and reflecting, to contemporary readers, some amusing prejudices.

It would seem that the author errs most in his estimates of the number of Germans who embarked for Louisiana and the number who actually arrived here. He states (pp. 16, 17) that: "... of those 6000 Germans who left Europe for Louisiana, only about one-third — 2000 — actually reached the shores of the colony... and were disembarked in Biloxi and upon Dauphin Island, in the harbor of Mobile ...", and (p. 23) "... It may be taken for granted that at these two places more than one thousand Germans died." Deiler based these estimates on authors such as Soniat Duffosat (Synopsis of the History of Louisiana), the Jesuit, Fr. Pierre Francois Charlevoix, and material in the possession of the Louisiana Historical Society. More recent research by M. Marcel Giraud, Professeur au College de France, into official records at Lorient, France, the port of embarkation of the Germans, indicates that Deiler's figures were overestimates. M. Giraud estimates that the number of emigrants was slightly over 1200 and that,

vii

of these, approximately 930 disembarked in the colony.

What is sometimes more frustrating is the haphazard arrangement of the material and the digressions into legends and material not germane to the topic. Deiler does not follow an orderly chronological pattern in tracing the German colonization of Louisiana but rather treats topics, individuals and episodes as they occur to him, as in the section (p. 66) where he interrupts the narrative dealing with the Census of 1721 to devote a chapter to Jean Daniel Koly.

The author's prejudices against Louis XIV (p. 14) and his jibes at Governor Bienville (pp. 69, 92) are amusing, and his commentary on the horrors of the Thirty Years' War (p. 14) in which, "... never before nor afterwards were such barbarous deeds perpetrated", certainly dates the book to the period before the great holocausts of this century.

But rather than berate the author for the book he did not write and for minor flaws, we should be thankful for the accumulation of facts which the book does represent. A major portion is devoted to the Census of 1724 and to the various German settlers mentioned in that enumeration, and, through the use of church records and official documents, an attempt is made to reconstruct for the record even those families which, for one reason or another, were not recorded in that census.

Three families are discussed in some detail: Zweig-Labranche (p. 101), Kleinpeter (pp. 108, 109), and Ory (pp. 110, 111), and many other families and individuals receive more than passing mention as the Index will attest.

I first became acquainted with The Settlement of the German Coast in 1958 when an initial curiosity about the origins of the Belsom family in Des Allemands led to the undertaking of what has become a research project of some magnitude on early German and French Louisiana colonial families. Since then I have frequently returned to Deiler as additional information was uncovered.

I was introduced to the task of indexing the book in January 1968 by local historian, Winston DeVille, whose own efforts in recovering colonial source material have been exhaustive. In approaching this undertaking certain decisions have had to be made. It was decided to record every surname which appears in the book, even in the case of variations in spelling of the original Germanic form of the name. This decision has greatly extended the length of the Index. Except where a specific individual is referred to in the text, references to a name have been indexed under the surname followed by "family". In cases where surnames are corruptions or variations in spelling of the original German surname that original surname is supplied in parentheses as an additional aid to the researcher. Thus, (p. 123) Quimel is indexed "Quimel family (Hymel) 123".

Whenever possible, full names are given in the Index, even when the reference in the text is to a surname only, thus, (p. 26) Governor Cadillac is indexed "Cadillac, Antoine de la Mothe, Governor 26".

Obviously there are some individuals who appear in the text under slightly different names but who are, in fact, the same person, thus, (p. 30) Zweig, Jean Adam and (pp. 85, 93) Zweig, Johann Adam, but, except in the case of obvious typographical errors, it was thought best to index the names exactly as they appeared in the text.

In indexing the brief genealogies of the Kleinpeter and Ory families and in a few other cases, it has been necessary to differentiate between several persons with the same name by the use of Roman numerals, I, II, III.

Finally, a Chronology of events has been added to assist the reader in relating the incidents mentioned by Deiler to the larger context of the colonial period in Louisiana.

The researcher interested in this area of history is referred also to the following sources for additional information on the German settlers in colonial Louisiana:

1. The papers of the author, J. Hanno Deiler, are housed in the manuscript collection of the Abbey Library, St. Joseph Abbey, St. Benedict, Louisiana, 70457.

2. The Louisiana State Archives and Records Commission has published as Volume III of its series, Calendar of Louisiana Colonial Documents, civil records of St. Charles Parish, Part I: The D'Arensbourg Records. This abstract of records of St. Charles Parish, prepared by Elizabeth Becker Gianelloni, covers the years 1734-1769 and includes marriage contracts, property sales, inventories and other civil matters. The Calendar may be purchased from the Louisiana State Archives and Records Commission, Baton Rouge, Louisiana. Xerox copies of documents listed in the Calendar are available from the Clerk of Court, Hahnville, Louisiana, 70057.

3. The remainder of the colonial records of St. Charles Parish for the years 1769-1804 are extant and are located also at the Parish Courthouse, Hahnville, Louisiana. However, to date no index or abstract has been done on these records.

4. The Louisiana State Museum Library, 547 St. Ann St., New Orleans, Louisiana has a photostatic copy of some of the earliest marriage, baptismal, and interment records from the Little Red Church, Destrahan, Louisiana, as well as a card file on these records. These earliest records evidently were not destroyed in the fire of 1877 mentioned by Deiler (p. 63).

5. The Genealogical Research Society of New Orleans in its quarterly New Orleans Genesis has published serially the above-mentioned Little Red Church Records. See New Orleans Genesis, January 1962, Vol. 1, No. 1, pp. 64-82 and subsequent issues.

6. In addition, the Society has begun the serialization of the Indexes of Marriages, Baptisms, and Interments of the St. Louis Cathedral,

New Orleans, Louisiana, in which are to be found many German surnames. See New Orleans Genesis, June 1966, Vol. 5, No. 19, pp. 188-217 and subsequent issues. Certified or, where possible, xerox copies of the original records are available from the Archivist of the St. Louis Cathedral, 615 Pere Antoine Alley, New Orleans, Louisiana, 70116.

7. Records of the 4th Judicial Court of St. Charles Parish, Louisiana, which are the Consentment of parents to intended marriages, beginning in 1816, appeared in New Orleans Genesis, March 1967, Vol. 6, No. 22, pp. 118-120 and subsequent issues. The St. Charles Parish Marriage Indexes, beginning in 1847, are appearing serially in New Orleans Genesis, beginning in September 1967, Vol. 6, No. 24, pp. 342-352 and subsequent issues. Descendants of many of the original German and Swiss settlers are to be found in these records. Xerox copies of these records are available from the Clerk of Court, Hahnville, Louisiana, 70057.

8. Finally, three Censuses have been reproduced in the pages of New Orleans Genesis: (a) Inhabitants of the German Coast dated 8 February 1749 which appeared in the issue of March 1968, Vol. 7, No. 26, pp. 146-149; (b) A Partial Colonial Census of St. Charles Parish dated 4 April 1766 which appeared in the issue of January 1968, Vol. 7, No. 25, pp. 30-34; and (c) General Census of the First German Coast, Province of Louisiana, dated 1 May 1804, which appeared in the issue of September 1967, Vol. 6, No. 24, pp. 337-340.

In addition to Winston DeVille, who provided both initial impetus and frequent counsel during this project, I should like to thank Rev. Pius Lartigue, O. S. B., St. Joseph Abbey, St. Benedict, Louisiana, and particularly Collin B. Hamer, Jr., Head Librarian of the Louisiana Department, New Orleans Public Library and his staff for their help and patience in making available to me on an almost continuous basis both Deiler's book and the space needed for spreading out index cards, proof sheets and the like. Naturally, any omissions or errors in the Index are solely those of the undersigned.

Jack Belsom

New Orleans, Louisiana

CHRONOLOGY

9 Apr 1682   Robert Cavelier, Sieur de La Salle, reaches mouth of the Mississippi River and claims Louisiana for France.

24 Jul 1684   La Salle's expedition sails from France to found a colony on the Mississippi River.

19 Jan 1685   La Salle's expedition lands at Matagorda Bay (Texas).

20 Mar 1687   La Salle murdered.

24 Oct 1698   Expedition commanded by Pierre le Moyne, Sieur d'Iberville, sails from Brest to establish a colony in Louisiana.

9 Feb. 1699   Iberville finds anchorage off Ship Island.

3-31 Mar 1699 Iberville ascends and explores the lower Mississippi River.

8 Apr 1699   Construction begun on Ft. Maurepas (Ocean Springs, Mississippi).

Jan 1702   Construction begun on Ft. St. Louis (Mobile Bay, Ala.).

24 Jul 1704   Le Pélican arrives at Mobile with 27 girls, the first females sent from France to the colony as wives for settlers.

Jul 1706   Iberville dies in Havana, Cuba. Jean Baptiste le Moyne, Sieur de Bienville, in command of the French settlement.

10 May 1710   Antoine de la Mothe Cadillac appointed Governor of Louisiana.

14 Sep 1712   Antoine Crozat appointed proprietor of the colony with exclusive trade rights.

Spring 1714   Louis Juchereau de St. Denis founds Natchitoches post.

26 Oct 1716   Governor Cadillac recalled. Jean Michiele, Seigneur de Lépinay named Governor of Louisiana.

6 Sep 1717   The Company of the West, headed by John Law, chartered.

20 Sep 1717   Lépinay recalled. Bienville again commander of the colony.

Spring 1718   Founding of New Orleans.

1718-1719   Arrival in Louisiana of over 300 concessionaries.

May 1719	Company of the Indies founded. Merger of Law's Company of the West with the Company of East India and the Company of China.
1719 (?)	Founding of the first German village (Le premier ancien village allemand) on the German coast by 21 German families.
18 Nov 1719	First mass arrival of German settlers at Ship Island on Les Deux Freres.
7 Jul 1720	First shipment of Negro slaves arrives in Louisiana.
16 Sep 1720	Arrival of Le Profond with German settlers.
9 Nov 1720	Arrival of La Marie with German settlers.
20 Dec 1720	Mississippi Bubble - Bankruptcy of John Law
24 Jan 1721	Departure from Lorient of German emigrants on four "Pest Ships": Les Deux Freres, La Garonne, La Saonne, La Charente.
3 Feb 1721	Arrival at Ship Island of La Mutine with German settlers and Swiss soldiers.
1 Mar 1721	Arrival of Les Deux Freres with German settlers.
4 Jun 1721	Karl Friedrich d'Arensbourg arrives at Biloxi on Portefaix with the last of Law's German settlers.
1721	Second German village founded on the German coast.
11 Sep 1721	Great hurricane floods German villages, damages New Orleans.
24 Nov 1721	Census of New Orleans and vicinity.
Jan 1722	Law's Germans from the Arkansas settle on the German coast.
12 Nov 1724	Census of New Orleans and the German coast.
15 Mar 1727	Étienne De Périer appointed Governor of Louisiana.
29 Nov 1729	Massacre of the settlers at Ft. Rosalie by the Natchez.
1 Jul 1731	Company of the Indies dissolved. Louisiana again a crown colony.
1732	Bienville again appointed Governor of Louisiana.
10 May 1743	Bienville replaced by Pierre de Rigaud, Marquis de Vaudreuil.
1751	Introduction of sugar cane into the colony from Santo Domingo.
3 Feb 1753	Louis Billouart de Kerlérec succeeds de Vaudreuil

	as Governor.
3 Nov 1762	Treaty of Fontainbleau. Louisiana ceded by France to Spain.
28 Feb 1765	Group of Acadians arrives in Louisiana from Santo Domingo. Other groups follow in May 1765 and in November 1766.
5 Mar 1766	Don Antonio de Ulloa, Spanish Governor, arrives in New Orleans.
28 Oct 1768	Revolt of the colonists against Spanish rule.
1 Nov 1768	de Ulloa, forced into exile, sails for Cuba.
24 Jul 1769	Governor Alexandro O'Reilly and Spanish fleet arrive at the mouth of the Mississippi to take possession of the colony.
25 Oct 1769	Execution of the patriots — Lafréniere, Noyan, Caress Marquis and Joseph Milhet.
1 Dec 1769	Luis de Unzaga replaces O'Reilly as Spanish Governor.
1 Jan 1777	Bernardo de Galvez succeeds de Unzaga as Spanish Governor.
18 Nov 1777	Karl Friedrich d'Arensbourg, Commandant on the German coast since 1721, dies.
1779-1781	Anglo-Spanish War. Governor Galvez and colonial troops defeat British troops and German Waldeck Regiment and capture Manchac, Baton Rouge, Natchez, Mobile, and Pensacola.
1 Mar 1782	Esteban Miró succeeds de Galvez as acting Governor.
1785	Importation to Louisiana by Spain of over 1600 Acadian refugees.
21 Mar 1788	Great fire in New Orleans (Good Friday fire).
1 Jan 1792	Francois Louis Hector, Baron de Carondelet, appointed Governor.
8 Dec 1794	Second great fire in New Orleans.
5 Aug 1797	Manuel Luis Gayoso de Lemos appointed Governor of Louisiana.
18 Jul 1799	Death of Governor Gayoso.
1 Oct 1800	Treaty of San Ildefonso. Louisiana ceded by Spain to France.
11 Mar 1803	Pierre Clément Laussat, Colonial Prefect, arrives in Louisiana.

30 Apr 1803	Louisiana Purchase.
20 Dec 1803	Laussat delivers Louisiana to U. S. Commissioners William C. C. Claiborne and General James Wilkinson.
26 Mar 1804	Congress establishes Territory of Orleans comprising the present state boundaries except for the Florida parishes.
2 Oct 1804	William C. C. Claiborne becomes Governor of Territory of Orleans.
Oct 1810	West Florida (Florida parishes) annexed to Territory of Orleans.
30 Apr 1812	Louisiana enters the Union as the eighteenth State.

CONTENTS

Contents

THE SETTLEMENT OF THE GERMAN COAST OF LOUISIANA

AND

THE CREOLES OF GERMAN DESCENT.

THE DISCOVERY OF THE MISSISSIPPI.

The first German upon the lower Mississippi was one of the last companions of the French explorer, La Salle. As the founding of the first settlement of Germans on the lower Mississippi also took place at a very early period in the history of Louisiana, we will first cast a glance into the history of the discovery of the Mississippi and the taking possession of the northern gulf coast by the French.

With the second voyage of Columbus (1493) and the discovery of Cuba, Hayti, Porto Rico, Dominica, Jamaica, and Guadeloupe, Spain had become the mistress of the Gulf of Mexico. Twenty years later Ponce de Leon came to Florida, and in 1519 Cortez began the conquest of the Aztec empire of Mexico. In the same year another Spaniard, by the name of Piñeda, sailed from Jamaica to circumnavigate Florida, which at that time was still thought to be an island; and as he always sailed along the northern gulf coast, he finally reached Mexico. For a long time it was believed that Piñeda on this voyage had discovered the Mississippi and called it "Rio del Espiritu Santo"; but Hamilton, in his "Colonial Mobile," maintains that the river discovered by Piñeda was not the Mississippi, but the Mobile River, and that Piñeda passed the mouth of the Mississippi without noticing it, it being hidden by sand banks, drift wood, and bushes.

In 1528 an expedition to Florida led by Panfilo de Narvaez failed, but, in April, 1536, four of its members, among whom was Gabeza de Vaca, reached Mexico by land after many years of wandering. These men must have crossed the Mississippi on their way to Mexico, and from their voyage and that of Piñeda date the claims of Spain for the ownership of the whole northern gulf coast from Florida to Mexico.

Induced by de Vaca's glowing descriptions of the country, De Soto, in 1539, began his adventurous expedition from Florida into the interior. About the 30th degree of latitude, he discovered the Mississippi (April, 1541) and found his grave in it; whereupon Moscoso, with the remnants of the expedition, floated down the Mississippi and reached the Spanish possessions on the gulf coast. This discovery was without any practical results, however, as no second attempt to reach the mouth of the Mississippi was made for the next 140 years.

Meanwhile the French had set foot on Canada (Port Royal, later called Annapolis, 1605; Quebec, 1608) and discovered the upper Mississippi. Many years, however, passed before La Salle, coming from Canada, followed the great river southward in its whole length, reached its mouth, and there, on the 9th of April, it "Louisiana," in honor of the king of France, Louis XIV. Then 1682, took possession of the Mississippi valley for France, calling he returned by the same way to Canada, and thence went to France to report on his discoveries and submit his plan to establish communication between Canada and the Gulf of Mexico by means of the Mississippi, and to secure the Indian trade of these vast regions by a chain of forts.

La Salle's propositions found favor with the king of France, and on the 24th of July, 1684, he sailed from La Rochelle for the Gulf of Mexico, intending thence to enter the Mississippi and to found on its banks a French establishment. He brought with him a flotilla of four vessels (Le Joli, L'Aimable, La Belle and a small ketch) under the direct command of Beaujeu. On this voyage a stop was made in the port of Petit Gouave in San Domingo, where La Salle was quite sick. San Domingo was then and had been for many years the headquarters of the buccaneers, whose calling was at that time considered a quite legitimate business, the riches of the Spanish silver ships and the many obstructions to commerce in Central and South America having, so to speak, provoked the other nations to smuggling and piracy. Merchants and many other highly respectable people of Europe furnished and sent out privateers, and rejoiced at their golden harvests. French, English and Dutch adventurers soon congregated in San Domingo, and these were joined by many Germans who had grown up in the wild times of the Thirty Years' War, and could not find their way back to peaceful occupations. In this company La Salle's men gave themselves up to riotous living, in consequence of which many fell victims to disease, and La Salle was compelled to enlist new men.

The First German on the Lower Mississippi.

Among the new men engaged in San Domingo by La Salle was a German, a buccaneer, an artillerist, who was known only by the name of "Hans;" *i. e.,* Johannes, John. The French wrote his name "Hiens," but Hennepin, a Dutch contemporary, calls him "Hans," and all agree that he was a German.

The record of La Salle's attempt to find the mouth of the Mississippi River from the Gulf of Mexico reveals a series of quarrels between the commanders, of misfortunes, errors and malice.

One of the four ships of his flotilla laden with thirty tons of ammunition and utensils and tools for his new colony, was captured by the Spaniards near San Domingo, because Beaujeu refused to follow the course recommended by La Salle.

The mouth of the Mississippi was not found by this expedition, principally because La Salle, on coming down from Canada and discovering it, in 1682, had committed the almost inconceivable mistake of ascertaining only the latitude of the mouth of the river, but not its longitude.

The expedition landed in Matagorda Bay, in Texas (February, 1685), where the frigate L'Aimable, on attempting to enter a river, was stranded. Joutel, an eyewitness, says:

"Circumstances reported by the ship's crew and those who saw the management were infallible tokens and proofs that the mischief had been done designedly, which was one of the blackest and most detestable actions man could be guilty of." (Joutel's Journal, Stiles, page 83.)

Then Beaujeu abandoned La Salle, left with La Joli for France, and took the crew of L'Aimable with him, thus violating his agreement with La Salle, and leaving the latter behind with the La Belle with eight cannon and not a single cannon ball. Finally, La Belle ran aground and was also lost.

La Salle then built a fort in Texas (Fort St. Louis) for the protection of his people, and from there made several attempts to find the "fatal river," as he called the Mississippi.

On one of these expeditions, which brought them up to the Coenis Indians, Hans, the German buccaneer, almost lost his life. They were crossing a river, when Hans, "a German from Wittenburg" (so Father Anastasius, a priest accompanying the expedition, calls him) got stuck so fast in the mud "that he could scarcely get out." La Salle named the river "Hans River," and in the accompanying map, printed in 1720, the name may be found inscribed in the French spelling "Rivière Hiens."

On the 7th of January, 1687, the last expedition from the Texas fort was begun. This was to be a desperate attempt to march with a picked crew of seventeen men from Texas overland to Canada to get succor, and on the way there to find the "fatal river." Among the selected seventeen was Hans, the German buccaneer, a proof that La Salle thought well of him. Twenty persons, among whom were seven women, were left behind in the Texas fort, where they eventually perished.

For several months this brave little band of seventeen men, marching again toward the territory of the Coenis Indians, cut their way through the wilderness, until they came to the southern branch of the Trinity River, where, owing to the tyranny of their leader, a conspiracy was formed among a portion of the men, and on the 18th of March, 1687, La Salle was killed by Duhaut, a Frenchman, who wanted to succeed him in the command of the expedition.

In this plan Duhaut, of whom all seem to have been afraid, was openly defied by Hans, the German buccaneer, and Father Anastasius, an eye witness, reports as follows:

"Those who most regretted the murder of their commander and leader had sided with Hiens, who, seizing his opportunity, two days after sought to punish crime by crime. In our presence he shot the murderer of La Salle through the heart with a pistol. He died on the spot, unshriven, unable even to utter the names of Jesus and Mary. Hiens also wished to kill L'Archevêque and thus completely avenge the death of La Salle, but Joutel conciliated him."

When the little band approached the French post on the Arkansas River, where, Hans thought, punishment was awaiting him for the murder of Duhaut, the German buccaneer resolved to join the Coenis Indians, whom he had helped to fight a hostile tribe; but, before leaving his companions, he demanded from them a Latin certificate to the effect that he was innocent of La Salle's death. This he received.

Only a few of La Salle's last companions reached Canada. Two of them, Father Anastasius and Joutel, published accounts of La Salle's last voyage, which have been followed in this narrative.

MAP OF LOUISIANA.

By J. Fried. Gleditschen's Son, Leipsic, 1720.

THE FIRST FRENCH SETTLEMENT ON THE GULF COAST.

Ten years passed before steps were again taken to found a French settlement on the northern gulf coast. In 1698, Iberville, a Canadian, sailed with four ships from the French port of Brest for the Gulf of Mexico. He found that in the meantime the Spaniards had taken possession of Pensacola Bay, for which reason he sailed further west, discovered Mobile Bay on the last of January, 1699, and, leaving his big ships in the harbor of Ship Island, went with two barges in search of the mouth of the Mississippi, which he entered on the second day of March. After ascending the river as far as the village of the Oumas, opposite the mouth of Red River, he sent his barges back to the mouth of the Mississippi, while he with two canoes entered Bayou Manchac, discovered Lakes Maurepas and Pontchartrain, and reached Ship Island by this route in advance of his barges.

Despairing of getting his big ships over the bar of the Mississippi, he resolved to make a settlement on the coast of the Gulf of Mexico; and on the 8th of April, 1699, active work was begun at the present site of the town of Ocean Springs, Mississippi, on "Fort Maurepas," the first French establishment in Louisiana.

The main settlement, however, was "Fort Louis de la Louisiane," founded in 1702, "sixteen leagues from Massacre (Dauphine) Island, at the second bluff" on the Mobile River.

"Sixteen leagues from Massacre Island at the second bluff is at Twenty-seven Mile Bluff. Near there Creoles still fondly point out the site of 'Vieux Fort,' and there French maps, as early as 1744, place a 'vieux fort, detruit.' A well under a hickory tree still marks the spot, and bullets, canister, crockery, large-headed spike, and a brass ornament were picked up by the present writer near the river edge of the level bluff as late as the summer of 1897. There, then, on a wooded spot, twenty feet above the river, hardly deserving the name of bluff, save above ordinary high water, was Fort de la Louisiane, commanding the wide, turbid river. It was not one of the many Forts St. Louis. Like Louisiana, it was named from Louis XIV., rather than for the sainted Louis IX." (Hamilton, "Colonial Mobile," page 38.)

In 1709 a great rise in the river occurred, which overflowed both the fort and the little town that had sprung up around it. A change of base was then decided upon, and "Fort de la Louisiane" was built on the site of the present city of Mobile. In 1710 the old fort was abandoned.

Here, at the old and at the new Fort de la Louisiane, or rather on Dauphine Island, at the entrance of the harbor of Mobile, where the large vessels from Europe discharged their passengers and cargoes, around the Bay of Biloxi and on Ship Island (Isle aux Vaisseaux) in the Gulf of Mexico, the life of the colony of Louisiana centered for the next twenty years. Here the principal events took place, and here also landed the first Germans.

On the accompanying map "Vieux Biloxi" means the old "Fort Maurepas," now Ocean Springs. Opposite is "Le Biloxi," the present Biloxi, Mississippi, or "New Biloxi," at first also called "Fort Louis."

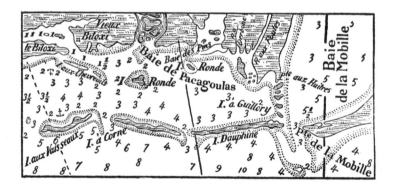

A GRAVE ERROR.

In the beginning of the colony the French committed the grave error of not giving any attention to agriculture. Two years after the founding of Mobile, in 1704, the civilian part of the population of Louisiana consisted of only twenty-three families, with ten children, who lived along the shore in huts with palmetto or straw roofs, fishing and hunting. It is true that they also had little gardens around their huts, but for provisions they relied on the vessels from France. They pretended that nothing could be grown on the sandy soil of the gulf coast, and they complained not only of the soil, but of the water also. Says Dupratz (1,268) :

"The soil and the water of Mobile are not only barren as regards the propagation of plants and fishes; the nature of the water and of the soil contributes also to the prevention of the increase of the animals; even the women have experienced this. I have it from Madam Hubert, the wife of the 'Commissionaire Ordonnateur,' that at the time when the French were at that post there were seven or eight sterile women who all became mothers from the time when they established themselves with their husbands on the banks of the Mississippi, whence the capital had been transferred."

The water and the soil of the gulf coast have not changed, and there is no complaint as to the birth rate now; considerable truck farming is done in the neighborhood of Mobile and on the back bay of Biloxi, and the Indians in the territory complained of always raised corn, beans, and many other things.

The truth is that the first colonists did not want to work, and the governors of that period complained bitterly of that fact. The people expected to find gold, silver, and pearls as the Spaniards had done in Mexico.[1] They also traded with Canadian "coureurs de bois," hunters who came down the Mississippi, killing buffaloes, and selling hides and beaver skins. The French also expected to do a great deal of business with the Spaniards in Mexico.

Since the expected mineral treasures of the gulf coast, however, have not been discovered even to-day—since the Spaniards, who claimd the whole northern gulf coast for themselves, were unwilling to trade with the French—since the trade with the Indians and with the Canadian hunters was too insignificant,—since France, whose treasury had been emptied by Louis XIV, could not do much for the colony—and, to make the worst come to the worst, since yellow fever was introduced from San Domingo in 1701 [2] and again in 1704,[3] the little colony of

---

[1] The name "Pearl River", which now forms the boundary line between the States of Louisiana and Mississippi, is attributed to the fact that some inferior pearls were said to have been found in that river.

[2] Sauvole, the first governor, died of fever in that year.

[3] The Chevalier Tonti died in Mobile of yellow fever in 1704.

Louisiana was for many years in a precarious condition and at times on the very verge of ruin.

Thus the colony continued until, in 1712, Crozat, a French merchant, took in hand its management as a commercial venture. He received the trade monopoly for fifteen years, but after the first five years he found himself compelled to ask the regent of France to rescind his contract, which request was granted.

THE "WESTERN COMPANY" AND THE "COMPAGNIE DES INDES"—JOHN LAW.

Then came, in 1717, the "Western Company," called after 1719, "La Compagnie des Indes," the leading spirit of which was the notorious Scotch financier, John Law. This company received the trade monopoly for twenty-five years. It was granted the right to issue an unlimited number of shares of stock, and the privilege not only of giving away land on conditions, but also of selling it outright. For these and other considerations the company obligated itself to bring into the colony during the life of its franchise at least 6000 white people and 3000 negroes.

The shares of the company were "guaranteed" by its assets. These were: first, the supposedly inexhaustible mineral treasures of Louisiana; secondly, the fabulous wealth of its soil, which was at that time not known at all, as "nothing could be grown on the sandy soil of the gulf coast," the only part then inhabited; and, thirdly, the immense revenues to be derived from the trade monopoly. In order to develop all these sources of wealth to their fullest capacity. agriculture was now also to be introduced on a grand scale. For this purpose large tracts of land, concessions, were now given to such rich men in France as would obligate themselves to bring the necessary number of people from Europe to till the soil.

One of the largest concessioners was John Law, the president of the company, who caused two concessions to be given to himself. The larger one was on the lower Arkansas River, on which he obligated himself to settle many people, for whose protection against the Indians he promised to keep a company of dragoons. His second concession was seven *lieues* below New Orleans, on the Mississippi River, below English Turn, and adjoining one of the concessions to the minister of war, Le Blanc, whose principal possessions were on the Yazoo River.

As a shrewd business man, which he no doubt was, John Law knew that, to make his venture a success, he needed not only capital but also people able and willing to toil for him; and, as he knew from the reports of the former governors how little adapted to agriculture the former French colonists had proven themselves, he resolved to engage for his own concessions Germans from the country on both sides of the river Rhine, and from Switzerland.

A great agitation was now begun, partly to induce rich people to take shares in the general enterprise and buy land for their own account, and partly to entice poor people to become *engagés* (hired field hands for the company or for the different concessioners). After a while, land was also to be given to the poor *engagés* to enable them also to get rich.

A German Description of Louisiana in the Year 1720.

About this time, pamphlets in several languages were printed, containing extracts from letters of people who had already settled in Louisiana, and giving glowing descriptions of the country. Such a pamphlet, in German, which, perhaps, came to Louisiana with one of the German pioneer families, was found by the author some twenty-five years ago in a little book shop in Exchange Alley, New Orleans, and at his suggestion it was bought for the Fisk Library, where it can be seen. It was printed by J. Friedrich Gleditschen's seel. Sohn, Leipsic, 1720, and bears the title:

Ausführliche
Historische und Geographische

Beschreibung

Des an dem grossen Flusse

MISSISSIPI

in Nord-America gelegenen herrlichen Landes

LOUISIANA;

In welches
die neu-aufgerichtete Frantzösische grosse

Indianische Compagnie

Colonien zu schicken angefangen;

Worbey zugleich
einige Reflexionen über die weit-hinaus-
sehende Desseins gedachter Compagnie,
Und
des darüber entstandenen

Actien = Handels

eröffnet werden.

Andere Auflage.
Mit neuen Beylagen und Anmerckungen
vermehret.

Leipzig bey J. Fried. Gleditschens seel. Sohn,
1 7 2 0.

After stating that "through the adventurer 'Christophum
Columbum' many of those Europeans had been led to leave
'Europam' for 'Americam,' especially for those then still un-
discovered countries," the author describes the boundaries of
Louisiana as follows:

"The boundaries of Louisiana are towards east Florida and Carolina, towards north Virginia and Canada. The northern limits are entirely unknown. In 1700, a Canadian, M. le Sieur, ascended the Mississippi over 700 miles. But there is still another district known of over 100 miles, for which reason it is almost to be supposed that this country extends to the 'Polum Arcticum.'"

The soil, the author says, is "extremely pleasant." Four crops a year can be raised. The abundance of the country cannot be easily imagined. There is also game, which every person is permitted to kill: leopards, bears, buffaloes, deer, whole swarms of Indian hens, snipe, turtle-doves, partridges, wood-pigeons, quail, beavers, martens, wild cats, parrots, buzzards, and ducks. Deer is the most useful game, and the French carry on a great "negotium" in doeskins, which they purchase from the savages. Ten to twelve leaden bullets are given in exchange for such a skin.

The principal things, however, are the mines:

"The land is filled with gold, silver, copper, and lead mines. If one wishes to hunt for mines, he need only go into the country of the Natchitoches. There we will surely 'draw pieces of silver mines out of the earth.' After these mines we will hunt for herbs and plants for the apothecaries. The savages will make them known to us. Soon we shall find healing remedies for the most dangerous wounds, yes, also, so they say, infallible ones for the fruits of love."

Of the spring floods in "Februario and Martio" the author says that they are sometimes so high that the water rises over 100 feet, so that the tops of the pine trees on the seashore can no longer be seen.

About New Orleans a man writes to his wife in Europe:

"I betook myself to where they are beginning now to build the capital, New Orleans. Its circumference will be one mile. The houses are poor and low, as at home with us in the country. They are covered with large pieces of bark and strong reeds. Everybody dresses as he pleases, but all very poorly. One's outfit consists of a suit of clothes, bed, table, and trunks. Tapestry and fine beds are entirely unknown. The people sleep the whole night in the open air. I am as safe in the most distant part of the town as in a citadel. Although I live among savages and Frenchmen, I am in no danger. People trust one another so much that they leave gates and doors open."

The productiveness of the investment in land, and the value of the shares are thus made clear to the people:

"If one gets 300 acres of land for 100 Reichstalers, then three acres cost one Taler; but, if the benefit to be derived and other 'prerogatives' of such lands are considered then an acre of this land, even if not cultivated, is worth about 100 Talers. From this basis it follows that 300 acres, which, as stated already, cost 100 Talers when purchased, are really worth 30,000 Talers. For this reason one can easily understand why these shares may yet rise very high."

No wonder that the agitation on both banks of the river Rhine, from Switzerland to Holland, bore fruit, and that thousands of people got themselves ready to emigrate to Louisiana.

Ten Thousand Germans on the Way to Louisiana.

German historians state that, as a result of this agitation, 10,000 Germans emigrated to Louisiana. This seems a rather large number of people to be enticed by the promoter's promises to leave their fatherland and emigrate to a distant country; but we must consider the pitiable condition under which these people lived at home. No part of Germany had suffered more through the terrible "Thirty Years' War" (1618-1648), than the country on the Rhine, and especially the Palatinate; and after the Thirty Years' War came the terrible period of Louis XIV., during which large portions of Alsace and Lorraine, with the city of Strassburg, were forcibly and against the protestations of the people taken away from the German empire, and the Palatinate particularly was devastated in the most terrible manner. Never before nor afterwards were such barbarous deeds perpetrated as by Turenne, Melac, and other French generals in the Palatinate; and whether French troops invaded Germany or Germans marched against the French, it was always the Palatinate and the other countries on both banks of the Rhine that suffered most through war and its fearful consequences; pestilence, famine, and often also religious persecution,—for the ruler of a country then often prescribed which religion his subjects must follow.

These people on the Rhine had at last lost courage, and, as

in 1709/10, at the time of the great famine, 15,000 inhabitants of the Palatinate had listened to the English agents and had gone down the Rhine to England to seek passage for the English colonies in America, so they were again only too eager to listen to the Louisiana promoter, promising them peace, political and religious freedom, and wealth in the new world. So they went forth, not only from the Palatinate, but also from Alsace, Lorraine, Baden, Würtemberg, the electorates of Mayence and Treves (Mainz and Trier), and even from Switzerland, some of whose sons were already serving in the Swiss regiments of Halwyl and Karer, sent by France to Louisiana.

The statement that 10,000 Germans left their homes for Louisiana is also supported by unimpeachable French testimony. The Jesuit Charlevoix, who came from Canada to Louisiana in December, 1721, and passed "the mournful wrecks" of the settlement on John Law's grant on the Arkansas River, mentions in his letter "these 9,000 Germans, who were raised in the Palatinate."

How Many of These 10,000 Germans Reached Louisiana?

Only a small portion of these 10,000 Germans ever reached the shores of Louisiana. We read that the roads leading to the French ports of embarkation were covered with Germans, but that many broke down on their journey from hardships and privations. In the French ports, moreover, where no preparations had been made for the care of so many strangers, and where, while waiting for the departure of the vessels, the emigrants lay crowded together for months, and were insufficiently fed, epidemic diseases broke out among them and carried off many. Indeed, the church registers of Louisiana contain proofs of this fact. In the old marriage records, which always give the names of the parents of the contracting parties, the writer has often found the remark that the parents of the bride or of the bridegroom had died in the French ports of L'Orient, La Rochelle, or Brest. Others tired of waiting in port, and, perhaps, becoming discouraged, gave up the plan of emigrating to Louisiana, looked for work in France, and remained there.

Then came the great loss of human life on the voyage across the sea. Such a voyage often lasted several months, long stops often being made in San Domingo, where the people were exposed to infection from tropical diseases. When even strong and healthy people succumbed to diseases brought on by the privations and hardships of such a voyage, by the miserable fare, by the lack of drinking water and disinfectants, and by the terrible odors in the ship's hold,—how must these emigrants have fared, weakened as they were from their journey through France and from sickness in the French ports? At one time only forty Germans landed in Louisiana of 200 who had gone on board. Martin speaks of 200 Germans who landed out of 1200.

Sickness and starvation, however, were not the only dangers of the emigrant of those days. At that time the buccaneers, who had been driven from Yucatan by the Spaniards in 1717, were yet in the Gulf of Mexico, and pursued European vessels because these, in addition to emigrants, usually carried large quantities of provisions, arms, ammunition, and money; and many a vessel that plied between France and Louisiana was never heard of again. In 1721 a French ship with "300 very sick Germans" on board was captured by buccaneers near the Bay of Samana in San Domingo.

After considering all this we are ready to approach the question of how many Germans really left France for Louisiana. Chevalier Guy Soniat Duffosat, a French naval officer who settled in Louisiana about 1751, in his "Synopsis of the History of Louisiana" (page 15) says, that 6000 Germans left Europe for Louisiana. This statement, if not correct, comes evidently so near to the truth that we may accept it.

To this it may be added that according to my own searching inquiries, and after the examination of all the well-known authorities, as well as of copies of many official documents until recently unavailable, I have come to the conclusion that of those 6000 Germans who left Europe for Louisiana, only about one-third—

2000—actually reached the shores of the colony.   By this I do not mean to say that 2000 Germans settled in Louisiana, but only that 2000 reached the shores and were disembarked in Biloxi and upon Dauphine Island, in the harbor of Mobile.   How many of them perished in those two places will be told in another part of this work.

FRENCH COLONISTS.

Besides John Law, who enlisted Germans, the Western Company and the other concessioners also carried on an agitation for the enlistment of *engagés*.   How this was done, and what results were obtained with the French colonists, is described by the Jesuit Charlevoix, an eye witness, who came to Louisiana in 1721 to report on the condition of the colony.   He says:

"The people who are sent there are miserable wretches driven from France for real or supposed crimes, or bad conduct, or persons who have enlisted in the troops or enrolled as emigrants, in order to avoid the pursuit of their creditors.   Both classes regard the country as a place of exile.   Everything disheartens them; nothing interests them in the progress of a colony of which they are only members in spite of themselves." (Marbois, page 115.)

The Chevalier Champigny in his Mémoire (La Haye, 1776) expresses himself stronger:

"They gathered up the poor, mendicants and prostitutes, and embarked them by force on the transports.   On arriving in Louisiana they were married and had lands assigned to them to cultivate, but the idle life of three-fourths of these folks rendered them unfit for farming.   You cannot find twenty of these vagabond families in Louisiana now.   Most of them died in misery or returned to France, bringing back such ideas which their ill success had inspired.   The most frightful accounts of the country of the Mississippi soon began to spread among the public, at a time when German colonists were planting new and most successful establishments on the banks of the Mississippi, within five or seven leagues from New Orleans.   This tract, still occupied by their descendants, is the best cultivated and most thickly settled part of the colony, and I regard the Germans and the Canadians as the founders of all our establishments in Louisiana."

Franz, in his "Kolonisation des Mississippitales" (Leipzig, 1906), writes:

"The company even kept a whole regiment of archers (bandouillers de Mississippi) which cleaned Paris of its rabble and adventurers, and received for this a fixed salary and 100 livres a head, and even honest people were not safe from them. Five thousand people are said to have disappeared from Paris in April, 1721, alone." (Page 124.)

And again:

"Prisoners were set free in Paris in September, 1719, and later, under the condition that they would marry prostitutes and go with them to Louisiana. The newly married couples were chained together and thus dragged to the port of embarkation." (Page 121.)

The complaints of the concessioners and of the company itself concerning this class of French immigrants and *engagés* were soon so frequent and so pressing, that the French government, in May, 1720, prohibited such deportations. This, however, did not prevent the shipping of a third lot of lewd women in 1721, the first and the second having been sent in 1719 and 1720.

Arrival of the First Immigration en Masse.

The first immigration en masse took place in the year 1718. There landed then in Louisiana, which at that time had only 700 inhabitants, on one day 800 persons, so that the population on that one day was more than doubled.

How many Germans were among these I cannot say; but, as several concessions are mentioned to which some of these immigrants were sent, and as the church registers of Louisiana mention names of Germans who served on these concessions, we may assume that there were some Germans among them.

In the spring and summer of 1719 immigration to Louisiana was suspended on account of the war which had broken out between France and Spain. The Louisiana troops took Pensacola from Spain, lost it again, and retook it. In front of Dauphine Island, in the harbor of Mobile, where there were some concessioners with their *engagés,* a Spanish flotilla appeared, shutting off the island for ten days. The crew of a

Spanish gunboat plundered the property of the concessioners lying on the shore, but were repulsed in a second attempt by the French solders, some Indians, and the people engaged by the concessioners.

In the fall of 1719 the French ship "Les Deux Frères" came to Ship Island with "a great number of Germans." The ship was laden with all sorts of merchandise and effects "which belonged to them." These people could not have been intended for John Law; for, judging from what they brought along with them, they must have been people of some means, who intended to become independent settlers.

A MISSTATEMENT.

This report is taken from "Relation Pénicaut." Pénicaut was a French carpenter who lived for twenty-two years (1699 to October, 1721) in the colony, and his "Relation" is an important source for the history of Louisiana. Mr. French, whose "Historical Collection of Louisiana" is well known, translated it and published it in the first volume of his "Louisiana and Florida." In this translation (N. Y., 1889, I., 151) we read concerning the German immigrants of the ship "Les Deux Frères," mentioned before, the following:

"This was the first installment of twelve thousand Germans purchased by the Western Company from one of the princes of Germany to colonize Louisiana."

This is not true. For in the first place, the original text of "Relation Pénicaut" which Margry printed in his volume V. does not contain a single word about an installment nor about a German prince who had sold his subjects to the Western Company; and secondly, people who come "with all sorts of merchandise and effects, which belong to them," are not people who have been sold.

In November, 1719, when the headquarters of the company were no longer on Dauphine Island, in the harbor of Mobile,[4] but had been again transferred to Fort Maurepas (Ocean

---

[4] A sand bar formed by a storm in 1717 having ruined the entrance to that harbor.

Springs), a part of this fort was burned,[5] whereupon the woods on the other side of the Biloxi Bay were cut down, and Dumont reports that "a company of stout German soldiers" were busy at that work. Whence these German soldiers came we are informed by the "Mémoire pour Duvergé" (Margry V., 616), where it is stated that a company of 210 Swiss "soldats ouvriers" had been sent to the colony. They cleared the land at the site of the present Biloxi, built a fort, houses, and barracks for officers and soldiers, magazines, and "even a cistern." This place was called "New Biloxi," and thither the Compagnie des Indes, on the 20th of December, 1720, decided to transfer its headquarters. Governor Bienville also took up his residence there on the 9th of September, 1721, but transferred it to New Orleans in the month of August, 1722.

From this time until the beginning of the Spanish period, in 1768, the Swiss formed an integral part of the French troops in Louisiana. There were always at least four companies of fifty men each in the colony. They regularly received new additions, and, at the expiration of their time of service, they usually took up a trade, or settled on some land contiguous to the German coast. It was even a rule to give annually land, provisions, and rations to two men from each Swiss company to facilitate their settling.

According to the church records of Louisiana (marriage and death registers), the great majority of these Swiss soldiers were Germans from all parts of the fatherland under Swiss or Alsatian officers. Of the latter, Philip Grondel, of Zabern, became celebrated as the greatest fighter and most feared duellist of the whole colony. He was made chevalier of the military order of St. Louis, and commander of the Halwyl regiment of Swiss soldiers.

As to the general reputation these Swiss-German soldiers established for themselves in Louisiana, it is interesting to read that

"Governor Kerlerec even begged that Swiss troops be sent to him in place of the French, not only on account of their superior

---

[5] A drunken sergeant dropping his lighted pipe had set fire to it.

discipline and fighting qualities, but because the colonists had as great a dread of the violence, cruelty, and debauchery of the troops ordinarily sent out from France as they had of the savages." (Albert Phelps' "Louisiana," page 95.)

In the beginning of the year 1720, says Pénicaut, seven ships came with more than 4000 persons, "French as well as Germans and Jews." They were the ships "La Gironde," "L'Eléphant," "La Loire," "La Seine," "Le Dromadaire," "La Traversier," and "La Vénus." As "Le Dromadaire" brought the whole outfit for John Law's concession, the staff of Mr. Elias,[6] the Jewish business manager of Law, may have been on board this vessel. For the same reason we may assume that the German people on board, or at least a large part of them, were so-called "Law People."

On the 16th of September, 1720, the ship "Le Profond" brought more than 240 Germans "for the concession of Mr. Law,"[7] and on the 9th of November, 1720, the ship "La Marie" brought Mr. Levens, the second director of Law's concessions, and Mr. Maynard, "conducteur d'ouvriers."

The Germans who came on the seven ships mentioned by Pénicaut and those who arrived on board the "Le Profond" seem to have been the only ones of the thousands recruited for Law in Germany who actually reached the Arkansas River, traveling from Biloxi by way of the inland route—Lake Borgne, Lake Pontchartrain, Lake Maurepas, Amite River, Bayou Manchac and the Mississippi River.

How the Immigrants Were Received and Provided for. A Terrible State of Affairs.

A rapid increase of the population, especially a doubling of it on one day, would at all times, even in a well regulated community, be a source of embarrassment; and it would need the most careful preparations and the purchasing and storing of a great quantity of provisions in order to solve the problem of subsistence in a satisfactory manner.

---

[6] Terrage calls him "Elias Stultheus".
[7] La Harpe.

On Dauphine Island and on Biloxi Bay, nevertheless, where the officials of the Compagnie des Indes ruled, nothing was done for the reception of so many newcomers. Everybody seems to have lived there like unto the lilies of the field: "They toiled not, neither did they spin." Nobody sowed, nobody harvested, and all waited for the provision ships from France and from San Domingo, which often enough did not arrive when needed most, so that the soldiers had to be sent out to the Indians in the woods to make a living there as best they could by fishing and hunting. Pénicaut says that the Indians, especially the Indian maidens, enjoyed these visits of the soldiers as much as the French did. This statement seems to be confirmed by the baptismal records of Mobile, where the writer found entries saying that Indian women "in the pains of childbirth" gave the names of the officers and soldiers whom they claimed as the fathers of their children. There are prominent names among these fathers.

Thus the poor immigrants were put on land where there was always more or less of famine, sometimes even of starvation, and where the provisions which the concessioners had brought with them to feed their own *engagés* were taken away from the ships by force to feed the soldiers, and the immigrants were told to subsist on what they might be able to catch on the beach, standing for the most part of the day in the salt water up to the waist—crabs, oysters, and the like—and on the corn which the Biloxi, the Pascagoula, the Chacta, and the Mobile Indians might let them have.

Governor Bienville repeatedly demanded that these immigrants should not be landed on the gulf coast at all, but should be taken up the Mississippi River to the place where he intended to esablish his headquarters and build the city of New Orleans; because thence they could easily reach the concessions, a majority of which were on the banks of the Mississippi. But the question whether large vessels could enter and ascend the great river—the French directors pretended not to know this yet, although the colony had been in existence for about twenty years—and the little and the big quarrels between the directors and the governor, whom they would never admit to be right, did not permit this rational solution of the difficulty.

Furthermore, as a very large number of smaller boats, by which the immigrants might easily have been taken to the concessions by the inland route through Lake Pontchartrain, had been allowed to go to wreck on the sands of Biloxi, the newcomers, especially those who arrived in 1721, had to stay for many months in Biloxi and on Dauphine Island, where they starved in masses or died of epidemic diseases.

It may be taken for granted that at these two places more than one thousand Germans died.

"Many died," says Dumond, "because in their hunger they ate plants which they did not know and which instead of giving them strength and nourishment, gave them death, and most of those who were found dead among the piles of oyster shells were Germans."

In the spring of 1721 such a fearful epidemic raged in Biloxi among the immigrants that the priests at that place, having so many other functions to perform, were no longer able to keep the death register. (See "Etat Civil" for 1727, where a Capuchin priest records the death of a victim of the epidemic of 1721, in Biloxi, on the strength of testimony of witnesses, no other way of certifying to the death being possible.)

Thus, for many months, the effects of the concessioners and of the immigrants were exposed to the elements on the sand of the beach. Even the equipment for Law's concession, which had arrived in the beginning of 1720, a cargo valued at a million of livres, lay in the open air in Biloxi for fifteen months, before the ship "Le Dromadaire," in May, 1721, at the order of the governor, but against the protests of some of the directors of the company, sailed with it for the mouth of the Mississippi.

This ship, with its load, drew thirteen feet of water and, as the "Neptune," also drawing thirteen feet, had crossed the bar of the Mississippi and sailed up to the site of New Orleans as early as 1718, and as an English vessel carrying 16 guns had passed up to English Turn in September, 1699, there was no reason whatsoever for detaining "Le Dromadaire" for fifteen months. A proper use of the "Neptune" alone, which had been stationed permanently in the colony since 1718, would have relieved the congestion in Biloxi and saved thousands of human lives which were sacrificed by the criminal neglect of the officials of the Compagnie des Indes.

As "Le Dromadaire" carried the oufit for the Law concession and for the plantation of St. Catharine, this ship may also have had some passengers on board, German *engagés,* so-called Law people; but perhaps not very many, as Bienville, in sending her to the Mississippi against the protests of some of the directors of the company, took a great responsibility upon himself, and could not afford to load her too heavily, lest there should be trouble in getting her over the bar of the river. The larger number of the German Law people, those who had arrived during the year 1720, had, no doubt, been sent to the Arkansas River by the inland route to clear the land and provide shelter for the great number of Germans who were expected to arrive in the spring of 1721.

No wonder that under such conditions as obtained in Biloxi a very low state of law and order reigned there, and that complete anarchy could be prevented only by drastic measures. A company of Swiss soldiers in the absence of their commander forced the captain of a ship to turn his vessel and to take them to Havana; and another company marched off to join the English in Carolina. The Swiss in Fort Toulouse, above Mobile, also rose and killed their captain; but these mutineers were captured and punished in Indian fashion by crushing their heads; one Swiss was packed into a barrel which was then sawed in two, and a German who had helped himself to something to eat in the warehouse in Biloxi was condemned by the Superior Council to be pulled five times through the water under the keel of a vessel.

But punishment which was meted out so severely to the small pilferer did not reach the guilty ones in high positions. Though the Germans on the other side of the bay died by the hundreds from starvation, Hubert, the commissioner general, who, as an investigation proved, had not kept any books during the whole tenure of his office, did not even know that there was a shipload of provisions in the hull of a vessel stranded near Ocean Springs and left there for eleven months. Yet Hubert was not punished.

Even this description, perhaps, does not give the whole truth, as contemporary writers did not dare to say what they knew. Dupratz says (I. 166):

"So delicate a matter is it to give utterance to the truth that the pen often falls from the hands of those who are most disposed to be accurate."

GERMANS IN PASCAGOULA.

In January, 1721, 300 *engagés* came to the concession of Madame Chaumont in Pascagoula. There were no Germans among them, as the census of 1725 shows, but Pensacola must be mentioned here, as there was a German colony at that place very early, arising, perhaps, on the ruins of this concession or of some other enterprise. The date of the founding of that German settlement is not known; but, in 1772, the English captain Ross found there, on the farm of "Krebs," cotton growing and a roller cotton gin, the invention of Krebs, and, perhaps, the first successful cotton gin in America.[8]

In the same year (1772) we hear of a great storm which raged most furiously "on the farm of Krebs and among the Germans of Pascagoula."

His last will and testament, written in New Orleans in the Spanish language in 1776, gives his full name as "Hugo Ernestus Krebs." He was from Neumagen on the Moselle, Germany, and left fourteen grown children, whose descendants still own the old Krebs farm, which the author visited in August, 1906. It is situated on a slight elevation on the border of "Krebs' Lake," near the mouth of the Pascagoula River, and a mile and a half north of the railroad station of Scranton (now incorporated with East Pascagoula), Mississippi.

---

[8] Cotton was planted in Louisiana much earlier. Charlevoix saw some in a garden in Natchez in 1721; and Dupratz constructed a machine for extracting the seed; but his machine was a failure.

The Creoles there call the Krebs home "the old fort," and the three front rooms forming the center of the house, the rest consisting of more recent additions, were evidently built with a view of affording protection against the Indians. The walls of this part of the house are eighteen inches thick, the masonry consists of a very hard concrete of lime, unbroken large oyster shells, and clay. The post and sills are of heavy cypress, which, after serving at least 175 years, do not show any signs of decay. The floor is made of concrete similar to that of the walls, but a wooden floor has been laid upon it, taking away about eighteen inches from the original height of the rooms. All the wood work was hewn with the broad axe.

In front of the house lies an old mill stone which once upon a time served to crush the corn.

Near the house is the "Krebs Cemetery," with the tombs of the members of the Krebs family, of whom a great number are buried there. The accompanying pictures were taken on the spot.

According to the family traditions the old fort was built by "Commodore de la Pointe," who is said to have been a brother of Madame Chaumont. Hamilton, in his "Colonial Mobile," page 140, says that Joseph Simon de la Pointe received, on the 12th of November, 1715, from Governor Cadillac, a land concession on Dauphine Island for the purpose of enabling him to raise cattle. As Dauphine Island was practically abandoned, after the great storm of 1717, de la Pointe probably also gave up his concession, and a map, drawn about 1732 ("Colonial Mobile," page 86) shows "Habitation du Sieur Lapointe" [9]) on the very spot where the Krebs homestead now stands, near the mouth of the Pascagoula River.

La Pointe's daughter, Marie Simon de la Pointe, became the first wife of Hugo Ernestus Krebs. Thus the old fort came into possession of the Krebs family, where it still remains, the present owner and occupant being Mrs. J. T. Johnson, née Cécile Krebs, an amiable and highly intelligent lady to whom

---

[9] Every concessioner was given the title of "Sieur".

THE KREBS HOMESTEAD (THE OLD FORT).

KREBS CEMETERY.

KREBS CEMETERY.

the author's thanks are due. She is the great grand-daughter of Joseph Simon Krebs, the eldest son of Hugo Ernestus Krebs and Marie Simon de la Pointe.

Francesco Krebs, the second son of Hugo Ernestus Krebs and Marie Simon de la Pointe, received Round Island in the Bay of Pascagoula, containing about 110 acres of land, as a grant from the Spanish government, on the 13th of December, 1783, after having occupied it for many years. The family of his wife had received permission to settle there from the French governor Bienville, who left Louisiana in May, 1743.

Pest Ships.

On the 3d of February, 1721, the ship "La Mutine" arrived at Ship Island with 147 Swiss "Ouvriers" of the Compagnie des Indes, under the command of Sieur de Merveilleux and his brother. French speaks of 347 Swiss.

Shortly before, on the 24th of January, 1721, four ships had sailed from the French port of L'Orient for Louisiana with 875 Germans and 66 Swiss emigrants. The names of these ships were "Les Deux Frères," "La Garonne," "La Saonne," and "La Charante." Of these four ships the official passenger lists, signed by the authorities of L'Orient, have been preserved, and a copy of the same came into the possession of the "Louisiana Historical Society" in December, 1904. From these it appears that these emigrants, who had, perhaps, traveled in troops from their homes in Germany and Switzerland to the port of embarkation, were divided on board according to the parishes whence they had come. Each parish had a "prévôt" or "maire," whilst the leader of the Swiss bears the title of "brigadier." We find the parishes of

> *Hoffen* (there is one Hofen in Alsace, one in Hesse-Nassau, three in Wurtemberg, also five "Hoefen" in Germany);
> *Freiburg* (Baden);
> *Augsburg* (Bavaria);
> *Friedrichsort* (near Kiel, Holstein);
> *Freudenfeld* (some small place in Germany not contained even in Neumann's "Orts-und Verkehrs-Lexicon," which gives the names of all places of 300 inhabitants and upwards);

Neukirchen (many places of that name in Germany, but this
   seems to have been Neukirchen, electorate of Mayence);
Sinzheim (one Sinzheim and one Sinsheim, both in Baden);
Freudenburg (Treves [Trier], Rhenish Prussia);
Brettheim (Wurtemberg);
Wertheim (on the Tauber, Germany);
Sinken (one Singen near Durlach, another near Constance,
   both in Baden, Germany);
Ingelheim (near Mayence, Prussia);
Hochburg (Baden).

It would seem strange that, in spite of the great number of
people whom these four vessels had on board for Louisiana, not
one of our Louisiana historians should mention by name the
arrival in the colony of more than one of these ships. There is
a horrible cause for this: *but few of these 941 emigrants survived
the horrors of the sea voyage and landed on the coast of Louisiana!*

The one ship mentioned as having arrived is "Les Deux
Frères," which La Harpe reports as having reached Louisiana
on the 1st of March, 1721, with only 40 Germans for John
Law out of 200 who had gone on board in France. The official
passenger list before me mentions 147 Germans and 66 Swiss, or
213 persons on board. *Therefore 173 lives out of 213 were
lost on this ship alone on the sea!*

And the other three vessels? Martin says that in March,
1721, only 200 Germans arrived in Louisiana out of 1200 embarked in France. Martin, no doubt, refers to the 875 Germans
and 66 Swiss on board the four ships just mentioned, with, perhaps, one or two additional ships.

"La Garonne" was the ship with the 300 "very sick" Germans which was taken by the pirates near San Domingo.

What suffering must have been endured on board these pest
ships, what despair! Fearful sickness must have raged with
indescribable fury.

The history of European emigration to America does not
record another death rate approaching this. The one coming
nearest to it is that of the "Emanuel," "Juffer Johanna," and
"Johanna Maria," three Dutch vessels which sailed from Helder,

the deep water harbor of Amsterdam, in 1817, with 1150 Germans destined for New Orleans. They arrived at the mouth of the Mississippi, after a voyage of five months, with only 597 passengers living, the other 503 having died on the sea from starvation and sickness, many also in their fever and utter despair having jumped overboard.[10]

There is a document attached to the passenger lists of the four pest ships from L'Orient, giving the names of sixteen Germans who were put ashore by the ship "La Garonne" in the port of Brest, France, a few days after her departure from L'Orient, and left at Brest at the expense of the company "chez le Sieur Morel as sick until their recovery or death." All sixteen died between the 10th and the 27th of February, 1721, proving the deadly character of their malady. This disease having broken out immediately after the departure of "La Garonne" from L'Orient, and evidently on all four vessels, we may assume that the passengers were already infected while still in port, and it must have broken out a second time on board "La Garonne" after her departure from Brest. The heartless treatment given the emigrants of that time, the lack of wholesome food, drinking water, medicines and disinfectants accounts for the rest.

Among the sixteen victims "chez le Sieur Morel" in Brest are found members of two families well known and very numerous in Louisiana at present:

> *Jacob Scheckschneider* (Cheznaidre) whose parents, Hans Reinhard and Cath. Scheckschneider, were on board La Garonne with two children;[11]
>
> *Hans Peter Schaf,* whose parents, Hans Peter and Marie Lisbeth Schaf, were on board the same vessel with two children. The whole family seems to have perished, but there was a second family of that same name on board which will be mentioned presently.

Of other passengers of La Garonne on this terrible voyage should be mentioned:

---

[10] See the author's *Das Redemptions system im Staate Louisiana*, p. 14.

[11] The surviving child, Albert Scheckschneider, became the progenitor of the Scheckschneider family in Louisiana.

Ernst Katzenberger and wife, founders of the Casbergue family;

Adam Trischl, wife and three children, founders of the Triche family;

Andreas Traeger, wife and child, founders of the Tregre family;

Jean Martin Traeger and wife, who seem to have perished;

Joseph Keller, wife and two children, founders of the Keller family;

Jacob Schaf, his wife and six children (probably related to the Schaf family mentioned above), the founders of the Chauffe family.

On the passenger list of the other three pest ships are found:

Heidel (Haydel) Ship La Charante. Widow Jean Adam Heidel and two children. They were two sons, the elder of whom, "Ambros Heidel," married a daughter of Jacob Schaf (Chauffe) and became the progenitor of all the "Haydel" families in Louisiana. His younger brother is not mentioned after 1727.

Zweig (Labranche) Ship Les Deux Frères. Two families:
1) Jean Adam Zweig, wife and daughter;
2) Jean Zweig, wife and two children, a son and a daughter. The daughter married Jos. Verret, to whom she bore seven sons, and later she married Alexandre Baure. The son married Suzanna Marchand and became the progenitor of all the Labranche families. "Labranche" is a translation of the German "Zweig" and appears in the marriage record of the son of Jean Zweig.

Rommel (Rome) Ship Les Deux Frères. Jean Rommel, wife and two children.

Hofmann (Ocman) Ship Les Deux Frères. Jean Hofmann, wife and child. Ship La Saone. Michael Hofmann, wife and two children from Augsburg, Bavaria.

Schantz (Chance) Ship Les Deux Frères. Andreas Schantz and wife.

These vessels having arrived in Biloxi during March, 1721, the 200 survivors of the 1200 Germans no doubt were in Biloxi in the following month, when the greatest of all epidemics raged there, and, after their escape from the dangers of the sea voyage, they again furnished material for disease. Jean Adam Zweig is especially mentioned in the census of 1724 as having died in Biloxi.

Towards the end of May, 1721, the "St. André," which

sailed April 13th, 1721, from L'Orient with 161 Germans, arrived in Louisiana. Among them are named Jean George Huber (Oubre, Ouvre), wife and child. A few days later, the "La Durance," which sailed April 23d, from L'Orient with 109 Germans, reached Louisiana. On the passenger list of this ship appears "Caspar Dubs, wife and two children." Caspar Dubs was the progenitor of all the "Toups" families in Louisiana. He was from the neighborhood of Zürich, Switzerland, where the "Dubs" family still has many branches in the Affoltern district.

Finally there came, according to la Harpe, on the 4th of June, 1721, the "Portefaix" from France with 330 immigrants, mostly Germans, and originally intended for John Law's concessions. They were under the command of Karl Friedrich D'Arensbourg, a former Swedish officer, then in the service of the Compagnie des Indes. La Harpe says that thirty more Swedish officers came with him.

CHARLOTTE VON BRAUNSCHWEIG-WOLFENBUETTEL.

A very romantic legend has come down to us from that time. It is said that with the German immigrants of the four pest ships who arrived in Louisiana in March, 1721, there came also Charlotte Christine Sophie, a German princess of the house of Braunschweig-Wolfenbuettel, who had been the wife of the Czarevitch Alexis, the oldest son of Czar Peter the Great of Russia. She is said to have suffered so much from the brutality and infidelity of her husband that, in 1715, four years after her marriage, she simulated death, and while an official burial was arranged for her, she escaped from Russia, and later came to Louisiana, where she married the Chevalier d'Aubant, a French officer, whom she had met in Europe.

Gayarré (Vol. I, page 263) made a very pretty story of this legend, and added a touching introductory chapter. According to him the Chevalier d'Aubaut, a young Frenchman, was attached to the court of Braunschweig as an officer in the duke's household.

"He had gazed so on the star of beauty, Charlotte, the paragon of virtue and of talent in her ambrosial purity of heaven, that he had become mad—mad with love!

Now the princess is on her way to St. Petersburg and her bridegroom is with her, and fast travelers are these horses of the Ukraine, the wild Mazeppa horses that are speeding away with her.

In her escort is a young Cossack officer riding closely to the carriage door, with watchful care and whenever the horses of the vehicle which carried Alexis and his bride threatened to become unruly, his hand was always first to interfere and to check them; and all other services which chance threw in his way, he would render with meek and unobtrusive eagerness; but silent he was as the tomb.

Once on such an occasion, no doubt as an honorable reward for his submissive behavior and faithful attendance, the princess beckoned to him to lend her the help of his arm to come down the steps of her carriage. Slight was the touch of the tiny hand; light was the weight of that sylphlike form: and yet the rough Cossack trembled like an aspen leaf, and staggered under the convulsive effort which shook his bold frame."

It was d'Aubant, of course, the Chevalier of the Braunschweig court, her lover in disguise.

"On the day of their arrival in St. Petersburg he received a sealed letter with two papers. One was a letter; it read thus:
'D'Aubant.

'Your disguise was not one for me. It could not deceive my heart. Now that I am the wife of another, know for the first time my long kept secret—I love you. Such a confession is a declaration that we must never meet again. The mercy of God be on us both.'

The other paper was a passport signed by the Emperor himself, and giving to the Chevalier d'Aubant permission to leave the empire at his convenience.

In 1718 he arrived in Louisiana with the grade of captain in the colonial troops. Shortly after he was stationed at New Orleans, where he shunned the contact of his brother officers and lived in the utmost solitude.

On the bank of the Bayou St. John, on the land known in our day as the Allard plantation, there was a small village of friendly Indians, and beginning where the bridge now spans the bayou, a winding path connected it with New Orleans. There the chevalier lived, and his dwelling contained a full length portrait of a female surpassingly beautiful, in the contemplation of which he would frequently remain absorbed, as in a trance, and on a table lay a crown, resting not on a cushion, as usual, but on a heart, which it crushed with its weight, and at which the lady from out of the picture gazed with intense melancholy. Every one felt that it was sacred ground out there on the Bayou St. John.

It was on a vernal evening, in March, 1721, the last rays of the sun were lingering in the west, and d'Aubant was sitting in front of the portrait, his eyes rooted to the ground—when suddenly he looked up—gracious heaven! it was no longer an inanimate representation of fictitious life which he saw—it was flesh and blood—the dead was alive again and confronting him with a smile so sweet and sad—with eyes moist with rapturous tears—and with such an expression of concentrated love as can only be borrowed from the abode of bliss above.

Next day they were married, and in commemoration of this event they planted those two oaks, which, looking like twins, and interlocking their leafy arms, are, to this day, to be seen standing side by side on the bank of the Bayou St. John, and bathing their feet in the stream, a little to the right of the bridge as you pass in front of Allard's plantation."

Such is Gayarré's account. It is a pity to destroy such a pretty legend, but the historian is not the man of sentiment—he seeks truth.

Let us examine this story critically, first acquainting ourselves with conditions in Russia, whence it emanated.

Alexis, the husband of the German princess, was at the head of the old Russian party which violently opposed the reforms introduced by the Czar Peter the Great, the father of Alexis. A conspiracy was formed by this party to frustrate the reforms, and the Czar, fearing for the success of his plans, forced Alexis, the heir apparent, to resign his claims to the Russian succession and to promise to become a monk. When Peter the Great was on his second tour through Western Europe, however, Alexis, with the aid of his party, escaped and fled to Austria. Very unwisely he allowed himself to be persuaded by Privy Counsellor Tolstoi to return from Vienna to Russia, whereupon those who had aided him suffered severe punishment, and Alexis himself was condemned to death. It is true, the sentence was commuted by the Czar, but Alexis died, in 1718, from mental anguish, it was said, but according to others he was beheaded in the prison. To meet the accusations of unjust treatment of his son, the Czar published the records of the court proceedings, proving the conspiracy.

There can be no doubt that the enemies of the Czar, especially the very strong and influential old Russian party, did everything in their power to make the treatment Alexis had received at the hands of his father appear as one of the blackest crimes, and that the Czar's party retaliated by blackening the character of the Czarevitch as much as lay in their power.

At that time, and for the purpose of defaming the character of the dead prince, the story that the German princess, his wife, had simulated death to escape from the martyrdom of a supposedly wretched married life, must have been invented by the partisans of the Czar. Why should she have gone to Louisiana, and nowhere else? Because everybody went to Louisiana at that time. It was the year 1718. That was the very time when John Law and the Western Company were spreading their Louisiana pamphlets broadcast over Europe; it was the time when thousands of the countrymen of the dead princess were preparing themselves to emigrate to the paradise on the Mississippi; it was the time when the name of Louisiana was in the mouth of every one. Moreover, Louisiana was at a safe distance—far enough away to discourage any attempt to disprove the story.

The tale, too, was repeated with such persistency that many European authors printed it, that thousands believed it, and that even official inquiries seem to have been instituted.

As to the princess' alleged Louisiana husband, the Chevalier d'Aubant, who was said to have married her in New Orleans in March, 1721, the present writer desires to say that he has carefully and repeatedly examined the marriage records of New Orleans, Mobile and Biloxi from 1720 to 1730 without meeting with such a name, or any name similar to it. Moreover, Mr. Hamilton, of Mobile, the author of "Colonial Mobile," [12] who examined the Mobile records completely and with infinite care, found only a French officer "d'Aubert" (not d'Aubant), who, in 1759, thirty-eight years later, commanded at Fort Toulouse; but this d'Aubert was married to one Louise Marg. Bernoudy, a daughter of a numerous and well-authenticated French pioneer family of Mobile.

---

[12] See pages 89 and 164 of that work.

The story of the romantic Louisiana marriage is therefore without foundation, and so the legend is a myth, although Allard's plantation, near New Orleans, is pointed out to us as the dwelling place of the lovers, and the two "leaflocked oak trees right by the bridge still bear witness to their happiness."

Pickett, in his "History of Alabama," claims the couple as residents of Mobile. Zschokke, the German novelist, makes them residents of "Christinental on the Red River," and others place them in the Illinois district; *i. e.,* the country north of the Yazoo River.

Martin says the King of Prussia called Charlotte's alleged lover "Maldeck." How the King of Prussia was hauled into the story can easily be explained. Louisiana was a French province, and (as will be shown in the chapter "Koly") the Prussian ambassador at the court of France was either for his own account, or as a representative of his king, financially interested in the St. Catherine enterprise in Louisiana; and he was therefore believed to be in a better position and nearer to the channels of information to make inquiries about affairs and people in Louisiana than any other German official in Paris. If, therefore, the family of Braunschweig-Wolfenbuettel desired to investigate the rumors current at that time, they had no better means of doing so than to request the King of Prussia to instruct his ambassador in Paris to make researches. The Prussian ambassador possibly reported that there was a man in Louisiana, by the name of "Maldeck" who claimed his wife to be the princess.

As to the name of "Maldeck," the writer will say that he found that name, or, rather, a name so similar to it that it may have stood for the same. In the passenger lists received by the "Louisiana Historical Society" from Paris in 1904 (see page 106), a laborer named "Guillaume Madeck" is mentioned, a passenger on the ship "Le Profond," who, from the 8th of May, 1720, to the 9th of June, 1720, the day of the departure of the vessel for Louisiana, had received thirty-three rations. A man of such humble station, however, would certainly not have suited a princess for a husband, and so, if the story was ever circulated in Louisiana, either Wilhelm Maldeck, or his Louisiana wife, claiming to be a princess, must have imposed upon the people.

JOHN LAW, A BANKRUPT AND A FUGITIVE.[13]

With the ship "Portefaix," so La Harpe informs us, the news of the failure of John Law and his flight from Paris reached the colony of Louisiana.[14] The news of Law's flight seems to have paralyzed the Compagnie des Indes, for it took them many months to decide what should be done with Law's concessions on the Arkansas River and below English Turn. The German *engagés* on the Arkansas River, who probably arrived there about the end of 1720, or in the spring of 1721, had not yet been able to make a crop, as the preparatory work of clearing the ground and providing shelter for themselves had occupied most of their time, and much sickness also prevailing among them, they were unable to begin farming operations on a larger scale before August, 1721.

These Germans therefore needed assistance until they could help themselves, for not another livre was to be expected from the bankrupt John Law; and the concession must be given up unless the company or some one else should step in to provide for those people.

It seems incomprehensible that the directors of the company in Louisiana, under these circumstances, should have waited from the 4th of June to beyond the middle of November of the same year to decide to take Law's concessions over; and even after they had decided to manage the concessions in the future for their own account, the resolution was not carried out, as Law's agent on the Arkansas, Levens, refused to transfer the

---

[13] Law left Paris on the 10th of December, 1720, for one of his estates six miles distant. There Madame Brié lent him her coach, and the Regent furnished the relays and four of his men for an escort. Thus Law travelled towards the Belgian frontier. Returning her coach, Law sent the lady a letter containing a ring valued at 100,000 livres. (Schuetz, *Leben und Charakter der Elisabeth Charlotte, Herzogin von Orleans*, Leipzig, 1820.)

[14] This statement of La Harpe cannot be accepted as correct. Law left France about the middle of December and the news of his flight spread rapidly. The ship La Mutine arrived in Louisiana on the 3d of February; the four pest ships which sailed from L'Orient on the 24th of January—six weeks after Law's flight—arrived in March; the ship St. André, which sailed April 13th, came towards the end of May, and a few days later came La Durance, which sailed April 23d, and still no news of the disaster? The ship Portefaix with D'Arensbourg on board, which arrived on the 4th of June, may have brought some instructions concerning the steps to be taken in the matter, but the first news must have reached the colony much earlier.

business to the company or to continue it in the company's name. Furthermore, as this man, in spite of his refusal to carry out orders, was left undisturbed in his position,[15] it happened that the German *engagés* in the meantime received help neither from one side nor from the other to bridge them over to the harvesting time of their first crop, but were forced to ask help of their only friends, the Arkansas and the Sothui Indians. Finally, when help from this last source failed, and small-pox broke out among the Indians and the Germans, they were forced to give up all and abandon the concession.

THE GERMANS LEAVE LAW'S CONCESSIONS EN MASSE, APPEAR IN NEW ORLEANS, AND DEMAND PASSAGE FOR EUROPE.

According to tradition, the Germans on the Arkansas re-solved [16] to abandon Law's concession and to go down the Mississippi to New Orleans. Only forty-seven persons remained behind, whom La Harpe met there on the 20th of March, 1722, when he installed Dudemaine Dufresne, but when La Harpe returned from his other mission, viz., the search for the imaginary "Smaragd Rock" in Arkansas, these too had departed.

The arrival of the flotilla of the Germans from the Arkansas River must have been a great surprise for the people of New Orleans. This city was at that time in its very infancy, and seems to have looked more like a mining camp than a town. The engineer Pauget, who went there in March, 1721, to lay out the streets, found in the bush only a small number of huts covered with palmetto leaves or cypress bark; and the Jesuit Charlevoix wrote from New Orleans on the 10th of January, 1722, *i. e.,* immediately before the arrival of the Germans from the Arkansas, that New Orleans was a wild, lonely place of about a hundred huts, and almost completely covered by trees and bushes. He found two or three houses, it is true, but such as would not have been a credit to any French village, a large wooden warehouse, and a miserable store, one-half of which had been lent to the Lord for religious services; but, he said, the

---

[15] He was replaced only in March, 1722, by Dudemaine Dufresne.
[16] It seems to have been at the end of January or in February, 1722.

people want the Lord to move out again and to accept shelter in a tent. Indeed, New Orleans contained at the taking of the census of November 24th, 1721, excluding soldiers and sailors, only 169 white persons, and the Germans who came down from the Arkansas must have outnumbered them considerably.

The surprise created by their arrival must have been a very unpleasant one for the officials of the Compagnie des Indes. Indeed, the Germans did not come to thank them for favors, and is it to be imagined that some very plain words were spoken by the Germans to the officials of the company; in fact, it is said that Governor Bienville interceded, and when they demanded passage back to Europe, tried his best to induce them to remain.

The results of the conferences were: first, that the Germans from the Arkansas were now given rich alluvial lands on the right bank of the Mississippi River about twenty-five miles above New Orleans, on what is now known as "the German Coast," comprising the parishes of St. Charles and St. John the Baptist, where, in 1721, two German villages, of which we shall hear more, already existed; secondly, that the agent on the Arkansas, Levens, was deposed; and, thirdly, that provisions were sent to the Germans who still remained there.

THE FAMILY OF D'ARENSBOURG.

The family of Charles Fred. D'Arensbourg is very important in the history of the German Coast, and as doubts existed until now as to its real descent, it will be treated here at some length.

The former Swedish officer who had charge of the German immigrants of the ship "Portefaix" and who became the commander of the German Coast, signed his name:

and the tradition among his descendants is that he was a nobleman.

Examining his signature, we notice at the end of the first letter a decided downward stroke, making it appear as if this downward stroke was intended to serve as an apostrophe, and that the man really intended to write "D'arensbourg", a form of name which would support the tradition of noble lineage.

The names of the older nobility being usually names of places, we shall now consider the only two places by the name of "Arensburg", which exist in Europe: one in the principality of Schaumburg-Lippe, Germany, and the other on the island of Oesel in the Bay of Riga, province of Livonia, Russia. As the principality of Schaumburg-Lippe is in Germany, and as the Russian province of Livonia was founded by Germans at Riga, in 1200, and belonged to the territory of the "German Knights" for centuries, and as the nobility of Livonia and the other Baltic provinces have kept their German blood pure to the present day, a noble family of that name would in either case be of the German nobility, and the original form of the name would be "von Arensburg".

As our Louisiana D'Arensbourg was a former Swedish officer, and as the town of Arensburg on the island of Oesel in the Bay of Riga, together with the whole province of Livonia, belonged to Sweden up to the year 1721, the year of Chas. Fred. D'Arensbourg's emigration to Louisiana, and as thirty other Swedish officers are said to have come with him to Louisiana in 1721, it might be assumed that our Louisiana D'Arensbourg belonged to the Riga branch of the German noble family "von Arensburg", and that, at the cession of Livonia to Russia, in 1721, our D'Arensbourg, together with thirty compatriots, who all had fought on the Swedish side against Russia, preferred exile to Russification, and emigrated to Louisiana in the year 1721.

Wishing to obtain more definite, and, if possible, official information as to the descent of this D'Arensbourg, the present writer addressed the Imperial German Consul in Riga, and this gentleman, "Herr Generalconsul Dr. Ohneseit", kindly submitted the questions to the chancellory of the "Livlaendische Ritterschaft, Ritterhaus, Riga", where the resident "Landrat" ordered researches with the result that the name of "von Arensburg" could be found neither in the church records of Livonia nor in the records of the "Livlaendische Hofgericht", to whose jurisdiction the island of Oesel belonged during the Swedish dominion and even later. Both the archivist and the notary of the "Livlaendische Ritterschaft" write furthermore that no family by the name of "von Arensburg" can be found in the literature relating to the Swedish, the Baltic, the Finnish or the German nobility. This settles the question of noble lineage.

"Herr von Bruningh," the archivist of the "Ritterschaft," however, agrees with the author, that "D'Arensbourg" points to the island of Oesel as the home of the man. It was also suggested that the man may have added "d'Arensbourg" to his family name (which must have been "Karl Friedrich") in order to indicate his birth place, or place of last residence or garrison, or in order to distinguish his family (there being many Friedrichs) from other branches of the same name, "which was not seldom done." Indeed, there were even several Friedrich families in Louisiana, and the census of 1724 mentions two of them, Nos. 2 and 42 in that census. In this case the change of name must have taken place before the departure from France, since the commission held by the Swedish officer was issued in the name of "Charles Fred. D'Arensbourg."

The following is offered as a possible solution: The former Swedish officer "Karl Friedrich," a German and a native or former resident of Arensburg on the island of Oesel, having determined to emigrate to Louisiana rather than become a Russian subject, applied to the Compagnie des Indes for a position in the colony, and in his petition, written in French, signed his name "Charles Friedrich," and added to it "d'Arensbourg" to indicate his birthplace, or place of last residence or garrison. The French officials, mistaking "d'Arensbourg" for his family name, issued his commission to "Charles Frederic d'Arensbourg;" and it being thus entered on the books of the company, and the man being known and addressed officially in that way, he was forced to adopt this as his family name.

The wife of D'Arensbourg, too, is said to have been a

Swedish lady, and her name, according to our historians, was "Catherine Mextrine." This is surely an error, for the author finds that D'Arensbourg was a single man when he came to Louisiana, in 1721. At least the census of 1724 mentions him as a bachelor, aged thirty-one, though the census of 1726 reports him as having a wife and one child. D'Arensbourg was, therefore, married in Louisiana, and we shall prove that his wife's name was neither "Catherine" nor "Mextrine," and that she was not from Sweden, but from "Schwaben" (Würtemberg).

The last three letters "ine" of the name "Mextrine" alone betray her as a German woman. It is the suffix "in," which was formerly added to the family names of married ladies in Germany. We had a German poetess by the name of "Karschin," the wife of a tailor named "Karsch;" the wife of a Mr. Meyer used to be called "Frau Meyerin," and I still remember that old people used to call my good mother "Frau Deilerin."

The French officials in Louisiana used to add an "e" to the "in" in order to retain the German pronunciation of the suffix. Thus the church records of Louisiana have:

Folsine, *i. e.*, the wife of Foltz,
Lauferine, *i. e.*, the wife of Laufer, and
Chefferine, *i. e.*, the wife of Schaefer.

The "x" in Mextrine is a makeshift for the German hissing sound of "z" or "tz," for which there is no special sign in French, "z" in French sounding always like a soft "s."

In proof of all this a facsimile of the signature of "Catherine Mextrine" is given here, which the author found in the marriage contract entered into between her granddaughter, Marie de la Chaise, and François Chauvin de Lery on the 23d of July, 1763:

It will be noticed that she signed her name without the final French "e," just as a German woman of that time would have written the feminine form of the name "Metzer."

Her family name, then, was "Metzer," and according to family tradition she was from Wurtemberg. The present writer is inclined to think that she was the daughter of one Jonas "Mesquer" (French spelling), who, according to the passenger lists, sailed with his wife and five children on the 13th of April, 1721, on board the ship "St. André" from L'Orient for Louisiana.

In the marriage contract of her eldest son, who married Françoise de la Vergne on the 18th of June, 1766, the mother of the bridegroom is called by the French notary "Marguerite Mettcherine." Here we also have her Christian name which corresponds with the initial of her own signature. It is not "Catherine" but "Marguerite," a favorite German name for women.

Karl Friedrich D'Arensburg served for more than forty years as commander and judge of the German Coast of Louisiana, sharing alike the joys and hardships of his people, and on one occasion, at least, taking an important part in political matters.

It is the proper place here to mention the part he, then a man of seventy-six years of age, played in the rebellion against the Spanish in 1768.

Ulloa, the Spanish governor, who had come to Louisiana in March, 1766, to take possession of the colony in the name of the King of Spain, to whom France had ceded Louisiana in 1763, had found the population very hostile; and, as he had only ninety soldiers with him, he did not formally take possession of Louisiana, but requested the French commander to hold over and act under Spanish authority until more Spanish troops should arrive. This interim lasted until the 28th of October, 1768, when the people rose and Ulloa was forced to retire to Havana.

During this year Ulloa had taken from the Germans of the German Coast provisions to the value of 1500 piastres to feed the Acadians, who had but recently come into the colony, and were not able yet to sustain themselves.[17]

---

[17] On the 28th of February, 1765, 230 persons, natives of Acadia (Nova Scotia) arrived in Louisiana. They came from San Domingo, where they had found the climate too hot, and were in great misery. Their whole for-

Hearing of the ferment all over the colony, and fearing that the Germans might make the nonpayment of their claims a pretext to join the conspirators, Ulloa, on the 25th of October, 1768, sent a man by the name of Maxant with 1500 piastres to the German Coast to settle the indebtedness of the Spanish government.

In a letter dated Havana, December 4th, 1768, one day after his arrival from New Orleans ("Notes and Documents," page 892) Ulloa says:

"In the early morning after Maxant's departure Lafrénière and Marquis sent Villeré and André Verret in pursuit of Maxant to prevent the remitting of the money to the Germans, fearing that if he should satisfy them they might no longer have any motive to join the cause of the conspirators.

"Maxant arrived at the habitation of D'Arensbourg for whom I had given him a letter and when he delivered it to him he found him to be so different a man from what he expected him to be—in spite of his great age determined to defend liberty and neither wanting to be a subject of the king (of Spain), nor the country to belong to the king.

"Maxant was arrested by Verret on the place of Cantrelle, the father-in-law of another Verret and Commander of the Acadians, where he was much maltreated. Verret declared later that he received the order to arrest Maxant from Villeré, Lafrénière and Marquis."

Ulloa in this letter expresses the belief that D'Arensbourg had been influenced by his relatives, Villeré, the commander of the German militia, and de Léry, the commander of the militia in Chapitoulas. It is true that Villeré was married to Louise de la Chaise, and François Chauvin de Léry to Marie de la Chaise, both granddaughters of D'Arensbourg, that de Léry was a first cousin to Chauvin Lafrénière, the attorney general of the col-

---

tune consisted of only 47,000 livres in Canadian paper, which the people of Louisiana refused to accept. Focault demanded permission from Paris to reimburse them, gave them 14,000 livres worth of merchandise and provisions, and sent them to Opelousas and the country of the Attakapas.

On the 4th of May, 1765, 80 persons from Acadia arrived and went to Opelousas.

On the 5th of May, 1765, 48 Acadian families arrived and were sent to Opelousas.

On the 16th of November, 1766, 216 Acadians arrived from Halifax. They were sent to "Cahabanoce," the present parish of St. James. These were the ones who received the provisions which the Spanish government took from the Germans on the German Coast.

ony and orator of the rebellion, whose daughter was the wife of Noyan, the leader of the Acadians.

But it needed no persuasion to make D'Arensbourg take the stand which he took, for Ulloa himself had furnished more than sufficient grounds to make him do so:

Ulloa had forbidden the flourishing trade with the English neighbors (September 6th, 1766);

He had closed the mouths of the Mississippi, except one where the passage for vessels was most difficult and dangerous;

He had refused to pay the costs of administration since the transfer of Louisiana to Spain (1763), and wanted to be responsible only for the obligations incurred since his arrival (March, 1766), thereby repudiating the salaries of officials, officers, and soldiers for three years;

He had imposed crushing burdens on export and import—vessels from Louisiana must offer their cargoes for sale first in Spain, and only when there were no purchasers in Spain were they allowed to go to the ports of other countries, whence they had to return to Spain in ballast, for only there could they load for Louisiana;

And, finally, by ordinance published May 3d, 1768, he prohibited commerce with France and the French West Indies.

This last ordinance was the most terrible blow of all for the colony. The flourishing lumber trade with San Domingo and Martinique was ruined thereby, and, with the ports of France closed, and only those of Spain open, the Louisiana products were at once thrown into direct and absolutely ruinous competition with those of Spanish America; for Guatemala furnished better indigo, the Isle of Pines more tar and resin, and Havana better tobacco than Louisiana.

All this tended to depress prices for the Louisiana products. Furthermore, would the colonists find a market for their goods in Spain as they had in France? Louisiana peltries received in trade from the Indians, the chief staple of the Indian trade, had less value in Spain, because they were used less there than in France; and the industries of Spain, much inferior to those of France, could not furnish the colonists with the class of goods which they needed to compete with the English traders in the Indian trade. Add to this the uncertainty as to the fate of the French paper circulating in Louisiana, and it will be easily understood that values of all kinds depreciated fully fifty per cent.

In addition to these hardships it must not be forgotten that, if this ordinance had been put in force, every man, woman, and child in the colony would have been compelled to give up their beloved Bordeaux wine and drink the "vin abominable de Catalogne."

All these reasons combined were surely enough to determine D'Arensbourg, who before the publication of the ordinance prohibiting trade with France seems to have acquiesced in the Spanish dominion, to take the stand he took. Indeed he did not need the persuasion of his relatives. No other stand was possible.

It was on the German Coast that the Revolution of 1768 began. D'Arensbourg, the patriarch of the Germans, defied the messenger of the Spanish governor; and it was surely D'Arensbourg's word and D'Arensbourg's influence that enabled Villeré to march two days later with 400 Germans upon New Orleans where the Germans took the Chapitoulas Gate on the morning of October 28th. The Acadians under Noyan, the militia of Chapitoulas under de Léry and the people of the town followed; and on the morning of the 29th they marched upon the public square (Jackson Square) before the building of the Superior Council to support the demand of Lafrénière to give Ulloa three days' time to leave Louisiana. The resolution was carried, and the people greeted the news with shouts of: "Vive le roi"! "Vive Louis le bien aimé!" "Vive le vin de Bordeaux!" "A bàs le poison de Catalogne!"[18] Ulloa left on the 1st of November on a French vessel for Havana.

The success of the revolution was due chiefly to Lafrénière, the Canadian orator, to Marquis, a Swiss and the commander of the revolutionary forces, who wanted to found a republic after the pattern of Switzerland, and to D'Arensbourg and the German and the Canadian militia.

A few Spanish officers having remained when Ulloa sailed, and Ulloa's frigate having been left behind "for repairs," the colonists frequently gave vent to their hostility to the Spanish;

---

[18] Franz in his "Kolonisation des Mississippitales" (Leipzig, 1906).

and in December a petition to the Superior Council was circulated demanding the removal of both the Spanish officers and the ship. A resolution to that effect was adopted by the Council, but it was never put into effect.

Meanwhile the news expected from France, where a commission of prominent Louisianians had petitioned the king to take possession of the colony again, did not arrive, and the hopes of the leaders of the rebellion against Spanish rule began to waver. They did not wish now to risk an attack on the Spanish frigate, and when the Germans of the German Coast threatened to march again to New Orleans to drive out the Spaniards, Lafrénière himself became alarmed and persuaded them to desist.

On the 24th of July, 1769, the news reached the city that the Spanish general O'Reilly had arrived at the mouth of the Mississippi with large forces to take possession of Louisiana. Again Marquis called the people to the public square, and implored them to defend their liberties; and again the Germans from the German Coast entered the city to oppose O'Reilly's entrance. But most of the others had already resolved to surrender, and so the Germans too had to give up their design.

Six of the leaders of the revolution were condemned to death, among them Villeré, Lafrénière, Marquis, and Noyan. Tradition informs us that O'Reilly intended also to have D'Arensbourg included, but that the latter was saved through the intercession of Forstall, under whose uncle O'Reilly is said to have served in the Hibernian regiment in Spain.

D'Arensbourg was made a chevalier of the French military order of St. Louis on the 31st of August, 1765, and died on November 18th, 1777. His wife died December 13th, 1776. They left numerous descendants.

THE GERMAN COAST.

The district to which Law's Germans from the Arkansas River were sent after their descent to New Orleans begins about twenty-five miles (by river) above New Orleans, and extends about forty miles up the Mississippi on both banks.

The land is perfectly level; at the banks of the river, however, it is a little, almost imperceptibly, higher, because of the deposit the Mississippi had left there at every overflow. At a distance from one to three miles from the river it becomes lower, and gradually turns into cypress swamps, so that on each side of the Mississippi only a strip from two to three miles in width is capable of being cultivated. For this reason land there is estimated only according to the arpent river front, to each arpent front belonging forty arpents in depth. This is what is called in deeds "the usual depth." An arpent is about 182 feet.

Large dikes, called "levees," now restrain the Mississippi from spreading over the lands in time of high water; but as the sediment deposited continually raises the river bed, the levees, too, must be made higher and higher. They are now from twenty to thirty feet high, the celebrated Morganza levee measuring even thirty-five feet. On this account, only the roofs of two-story houses can be seen from the middle of the river.

The crown of the levee, where a delightful breeze is found even during the hottest part of the day, is from six to ten feet wide, affording, besides a beautiful view of the Mississippi and the vast area of level land back to the cypress swamps, a very pleasant promenade where the people love to gather.

Along the inland base of the levee runs the only wagon road up the coast,[19] and still farther inland, between majestic shade trees or groves, stand the palatial mansions of the planters with their numerous outhouses. Some distance in the rear are the sugar houses with their big chimneys; and from these a wide street, lined with a double row of little white cabins with two or four rooms each, leads to the fields. In the days of slavery this was the negro quarters, but now the free laborers and field hands, mostly Italians, live there.

The fields, whose furrows run invariably at right angles with the river, extend as far as the eye can see, to the cypress forests in the swamps. Every fifty or sixty feet a narrow but deep and well kept ditch runs in the same direction; little railroads lead from the fields, whence they carry the sugar cane to the sugar houses, and in the month of November, when the grinding

[19] The banks of the Mississippi River are called "coast." Hence the "German Coast."

season begins, these fields, with the waving sugar cane, afford a beautiful sight. Four important railroads, running parallel to the Mississippi, intersect the rear of the plantations, the Yazoo & Mississippi Valley and the Louisiana Railway and Navigation Co.'s line on one side of the Mississippi, and the Southern and the Texas Pacific on the other. Between New Orleans and Baton Rouge, the people plant mostly sugar cane, but also some rice and corn. Beyond Baton Rouge, cotton takes the place of the sugar cane.

In some places wide strips of torn up land, with hollows and trenches scooped out, and with little hills of deposit extend from the river to the swamp. These are places where the Mississippi has broken through the levee, its mighty waters rushing with a roar heard for miles down upon the land twenty or thirty feet below, wrecking houses, uprooting trees, carrying off fences, and inundating and devastating hundreds of miles of the richest lands.

Little crawfishes from the river sometimes crawl up to the base of the levee and work their way through the earth masses. The water follows them, and all of a sudden a little spring bubbles up on the inland slope of the levee. If this is not discovered at once by the guards watching at high water time day and night, it widens rapidly until the earth from the top tumbles down, and a "crevasse" results. However small this opening may be in the beginning, it will, through the crumbling away of both ends, soon extend hundreds of feet, and so great is the force of the current that even large Mississippi steamers have been carried through such breaks.

Woe to the planter who does not, at the first warning, flee with his people and his stock to some safe place on the crown of the levee where rescue steamers can reach them.

Sometimes also defective rice flumes, laid through the levee to obtain water for the rice fields, have caused crevasses.

On the left bank of the German Coast, between Montz and La Place, two stations of the Yazoo & Mississippi Valley Railway, such a strip of torn up land may be seen. Here was "Bonnet Carré Crevasse (April 11th, 1874) which was 1370 feet wide, from twenty-five to fifty-two feet deep and which remained open for eight years. Further up the river, and on the same side, near Oneida (Welham station of the same railroad) was "Nita Crevasse," which occurred on the 13th of March, 1890, and was 3000 feet wide. Both these crevasses did immense damage even to the German farmers near Frenier, more than ten miles distant from the break, where the crevasse water entered Lake Pontchartrain and washed so much land into the lake that houses which stood 150 feet from the shore had to be moved back.

This is the German Coast of to-day. At the time of the settling of the German pioneers, in 1721, it was quite different. There were no levees then, and the whole country was a howling wilderness.

This district was called "La Côte des Allemands," but usually only "Aux Allemands." During the Spanish period (after 1768) it was called "El Puerto des Alemanes," and when the district was divided there were a "Primera Costa de los Alemanes" and a "Segunda Costa." Since 1802 the lower part has been called "St. Charles Parish," and the upper "St. John the Baptist Parish."

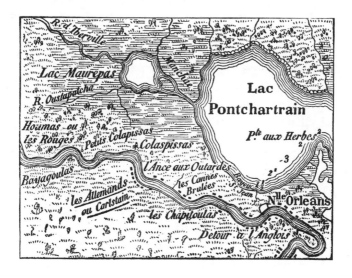

THE FIRST VILLAGES ON THE GERMAN COAST.

The weight of authority and tradition among our Creole population of German descent up to the present time has favored the legend that Karl Friedrich D'Arensbourg, who came to Louisiana on the ship "Portefaix" on the fourth of June, 1721, was the leader of the Germans already on the Arkansas River, and that he came down from there with Law's Germans to the German Coast.

Careful researches and the finding of new material until recently unavailable have convinced the writer that this legend can no longer be entertained. D'Arensbourg never was on the Arkansas River, and the Germans from there were not the first Germans on the German Coast. There had been established two German villages on the German Coast prior to the arrival there of the people from the Arkansas River.

Here are the facts:

The census of 1724, a most important document, a copy of which was received by the "Louisiana Historical Society" from Paris, in December, 1904, mentions two old German villages, ten lieues (about thirty miles) above New Orleans on the right bank. "Le premier ancien village allemand" was one and a half miles inland from the Mississippi, the second three quarters of a mile, and between the two lay a tract of four arpents of land, which had been cleared by the community to serve as a cemetery. When the census of 1724 was taken the people of the second village (the one nearer to the Mississippi) had all been three years on their lands. This throws the founding of the second village into the year 1721.

The first German village ("le premier ancien village allemand") *i. e.*, the one remoter from the Mississippi, was founded, so the census says, by twenty-one German families, but the time of the founding is not given. These twenty-one families must have come before the others, otherwise their village would not have been called "le *premier* ancien village allemand."

As Pénicaut informed us that in 1719 the ship "Les Deux Freres" brought a number of German people, "with all sorts of merchandise and effects which belonged to them," and as these evidently were people of some means, who wanted to become independent settlers, we may assume that they were the founders of "le premier ancien village allemand," one and a half miles inland from the Mississippi River. The census of 1724 informs us that the people of the first village, when they left their homes in consequence of the inundation of 1721, abandoned 100 arpents of "beautifully cleared lands." As it took time to clear these lands it is easy to see, that the first village must have been settled much earlier than the second.

In September, 1721, so the census of 1724 continues, the people of the two old villages were drowned out by the storm water of the "great hurricane," and the waters of the lake. This storm[20] lasted five days. The wind blew first from the southeast, then from the south, and, finally, from the southwest. There being large bodies of water in the rear of the German Coast, "Lac des Allemands" on the north, "Lake Salvador" on the south, and the "Bayou des Allemands" connecting the two, it must have been the waters of these which were hurled against the two German villages.

Over 8000 quarts of rice, ready for the harvest, were lost in this storm. In New Orleans most of the houses were blown down; in Biloxi the magazines were wrecked "to the great satisfaction of the keepers, this accident relieving them from the obligation of rendering their accounts." In Ocean Springs "one had the great sorrow to lose a great quantity of artillery, of lead, and provisions, which had been a long time on board a freight ship stranded near Old Biloxi, and which for more than a year they had neglected to put ashore." It will be remembered that during the summer of 1721, while these provisions were lying in the stranded vessel at Ocean Springs, the Germans on

---

[20] The year of the great storm is stated differently by Louisiana writers. The reason for this is the fact that several of the older authorities relied upon began to write their works many years after these occurrences, and, so it seems, partly from memory; and therefore confused dates in the retrospect. But the official census of 1724, having been taken but three years after the great storm, on the spot, and while everything was yet fresh in the minds of the people may be relied upon as absolutely correct. That part of the census reporting the great storm is dated September 12th, 1724, and says, on page 86: "Ils furent noyes il y a trois ans lors de l'ouragon par la pluye et par les eaux du lac que le vent jetta sur leur terrain quoy qu'ils en eloignez de deux a trois lieues."

the other side of the bay were allowed to starve by the hundreds.

According to the census of 1724, some of the inundated families of the two old German villages on the German Coast died, others moved to the river front, where the land was higher, and only three: Diehl, Schenck and Kobler, were found in "le premier ancien village allemand" by the census enumerator of 1724.

The second village, the one nearer to the Mississippi, was also partly abandoned, and the people from there also moved to the river bank; but fourteen households, including those of four widows, remained behind. On the river bank a new establishment was founded.

All this happened in the year 1721, when the Germans of Law were yet on the Arkansas River. It has, therefore, been proved that there were two German villages on the German Coast before the Arkansas people came down the Mississippi.

KARL FRIEDRICH D'ARENSBOURG AND THE FOUNDERS OF THE SECOND GERMAN VILLAGE ON THE GERMAN COAST.

Having ascertained now beyond a doubt that there were two German villages on the German Coast of Louisiana before the arrival of the people from the Arkansas River, and having ventured a suggestion as to the people who were the founders of the first village, we shall now attempt to answer the question: "Whence came the Germans who founded the second village?"

As has already been stated, the "Portefaix" arrived in Louisiana on the 4th of June, 1721, with 330 passengers, mostly Germans under the leadership of Karl Friedrich D'Arensbourg. Why this time a special leader for *engagés* if these were intended for John Law's concessions? Every concessioner managed his *engagés* through his own officers, and D'Arensbourg was not in the employ of Law, for his commission, issued January 9th, 1721, was not a commission by John Law, but by the Compagnie des Indes. Unusual conditions must have obtained to cause the company to send a special officer with these German emigrants.

La Harpe informs us that the same ship brought the news

of John Law's bankruptcy and flight from Paris. That Law was bankrupt and a fugitive at that time is a fact. He had fled from Paris to Brussels on the 10th of December, 1720. It is certain, therefore, that the Compagnie des Indes in Paris knew, in December, 1720, if not before, that there was no further need of sending people for Law's enterprises in Louisiana, as Law could not hold his concessions any longer, and could not support the people working for him in Louisiana until they could make their first crop to support themselves. The company, furthermore, knew that the sending of any more *engagés* for the Law enterprises would only increase its embarrassment and still more complicate matters on the Arkansas River.

What disposition, then, was the company to make of the many hundred Germans whom the agents of Law had engaged in Germany before the bankruptcy of their master, and who were now in the French ports clamoring for passage for Louisiana? There were only two ways out of the dilemma. Having these people on its hands and ready to sail when the catastrophe occurred, the company might decide to have them distributed among the other concessioners in Louisiana; but this would not have necessitated the sending along with them of a special officer, for the company's officials in Louisiana could have attended to the distribution. The company, secondly, might decide to keep the people together after their arrival in Louisiana, to organize them into a body, and to establish a new community with them. If this was the intention, then it was but natural to select as their leader and head an officer of their own nationality, a man speaking the German language. D'Arensbourg filled this condition, and, moreover, he was supposed to be a German nobleman, to whose authority the Germans would willingly submit.

At this point the date of D'Arensbourg's appointment assumes special importance. His commission was issued in Paris on the 9th of January, 1721, *i. e.,* shortly after the flight of John Law, and at the very time when the need of such a man was urgent. The writer is, therefore, of the opinion that the company, after the flight of Law, decided to send no more

Germans to the Law concessions in Louisiana, but to organize under the leadership of D'Arensbourg the Germans still in the ports of France, and to begin a new settlement with them somewhere in Louisiana.

Of the German *engagés* in the ports of France at this critical juncture, 875 Germans and 66 Swiss left France on the 24th of January, 1721, on the four pest ships spoken of on a previous page. Two hundred of them arrived in Biloxi during March, where their number was again greatly reduced by the terrible epidemic then prevailing.

Why D'Arensbourg was not sent with the first ships sailing after his appointment may be due to the fact that a stay of several months of these people in Biloxi was expected, and that D'Arensbourg's presence was not needed, as the company had its headquarters in Biloxi, and its officials there could take care of the Germans on their arrival in Louisiana. So D'Arensbourg brought up the rear, and came with the last troop on board "Portefaix," reaching Biloxi on the 4th of June and meeting there the sad relics of the pest ships and the few survivors of the epidemic, a number of them widows and orphans.

There is no doubt that a number of the passengers of the "Portefaix," too, succumbed to the epidemic which was still raging in Biloxi when that ship arrived, and that D'Arensbourg then, merging the survivors of the different troops into one body, departed with them for the banks of the Mississippi. Where he went to form a settlement the writer has been able to ascertain partly from the passenger lists and partly from the census of 1724.

Six out of the fourteen German families still found in 1724 in the partly abandoned second old German village, three quarters of a mile from the Mississippi, were survivors of the pest ships D'Arensbourg had met in Biloxi; and Schenck, Diehl, and Kobler, the three families which had moved from the second, partly abandoned, to the first, totally abandoned, village, had also been passengers on the pest ships. If the passenger list of the "Portefaix" were available, it would perhaps show that the remainder of the fourteen households of the second village consisted of passengers of the "Portefaix." Finally, D'Arensbourg's own land, twelve arpents, was between the two old German villages and adjoining the cemetery, which was midway between the villages.

All the people of the second village having been three years on their lands in 1724, (see census of that year) there can be no doubt that D'Arensbourg and his people settled on this place in 1721, and instead of going up to the Arkansas River founded the "second old German village."

When the first village and part of the second village were abandoned after the hurricane of September, 1721, and a new establishment was founded on the river bank, D'Arensbourg remained on his land between the two old villages; and when, after the completion of the new cemetery and the chapel on the river bank, Oberle and Hecker, two Germans from the second village, took possession of the old cemetery, D'Arensbourg, as judge and commander, claimed this land adjoining his own for himself on the ground that it had been cleared by the old community for a cemetery and was, therefore, public land.

According to a map of the year 1731 (Crown Maps) this chapel stood on the river bank, on the place now known by the name of "Le Sassier," or "Trinity Plantation;" and about one mile below the chapel, but on the opposite bank of the Mississippi, was a small military post with one gun mounted "en barbette."

The old villages, including D'Arensbourg's own land, had been called "Karlstein," no doubt in honor of the first judge and commander of the German Coast, Karl Friedrich D'Arensbourg, but the new establishment on the river front was given another name. There, in the new village on the river bank, the Germans from the Arkansas River, coming down the Mississippi on their way to New Orleans, must have met their countrymen; and this meeting must have been a great incentive for the Arkansas people to accept Bienville's offer of lands above and below the river front village of their countrymen on the German Coast.

This also explains why we hear from now on of three German villages on the river front, the village of the D'Arensbourg people in the center, and two villages of the Arkansas people, one above and the other below the first: "Hoffen," "Mariental," and "Augsburg." The name Karlstein was retained for the little settlement in the rear, and Karlstein being the name of the residence of the commander and judge of the German Coast, it gradually superseded all the other names. The little map on page 49 bears the inscription: "Les Allemands ou Carlstain."

HARDSHIPS AND DIFFICULTIES ENCOUNTERED BY THE GERMAN PIONEERS.

No pen can describe, nor human fancy imagine the hardships which the German pioneers of Louisiana suffered even after they had survived the perils of the sea, and epidemics and starvation on the sands of Biloxi. No wonder that so many perished. Had they been of a less hardy race, not one of these families would have survived.

It should be remembered that the land assigned to them was virgin forest in the heavy alluvial bottoms of the Mississippi, with their tremendous germinating powers awakened by a semitropical sun. Giant oaks with wide-spreading arms and gray mossy beards stood there as if from eternity, and defied the axe of man. Between them arose towering pines with thick undergrowth, bushes and shrubs and an impenetrable twist of running, spinning, and climbing vines, under whose protection lurked a hell of hostile animals and savage men. Leopards, bears, panthers, wild cats, snakes, and alligators, and their terrible allies, a scorching sun, the miasma rising from the disturbed virgin soil, and the floods of a mighty river,—all these combined to destroy the work of man and man himself. There were no levees then, no protecting dams, and only too often when the spring floods came, caused by the simultaneous melting of the snow in the vast region of the upper course of the Mississippi and its tributaries, the colonists were driven to climb upon the roofs of their houses, and up into the trees, and hundreds of miles of fertile lands were inundated.

MISSISSIPPI LEVEE IN FRONT OF ST. JOHN THE BAPTIST CHURCH
"AUX ALLEMANDS."

The following petition, perhaps one of many similar ones in that year, the author found among official acts:

"A MESSIEURS DU CONSEIL SUPERIEUR DE LA NOUVELLE REGIE.

Le nomme Jean Jacob Foltz habitant allemand, prend la liberté de vous representer tres humblement, que l'année passée il auroit esté innondée sur son habitation par le Mississippi, de sorte qu'apres avoir travaillée pandant tout l'année il na peu recoultire que sept bary de Ris, et se trouvent aujourdhuy dans la dernier necessitét aveque une femme et un enfant, c'est pour ce donc il requet

Ce consideré messieurs il vous plaise de luy accorder quelque quart de Ris pour pouvoir subsister aveque sa famille jusque' a sa recolte, les quelles il s'oblige de rendre a la dite recolte. C'est la Grace qu'ill espere de vos bontets ordinaires, il priras Dieu pour votre Santé et prosperitet, a la Nouvelle Orleans, 12 May, 1725.

(Signed) Jacob Foltz.

The petitioner informs the Superior Council that his place had been inundated by the Mississippi in the preceding year, and to such an extent that, after a whole year's work, he had been able to harvest only seven barrels of rice, and that he finds himself now with his family, consisting of his wife and a child, in the direst need. For this reason he petitions the Council to advance him some rice so that he may be able to sustain his family until next harvest, when he promises to pay back the rice advanced to him. According to a note on the margin of the document, the prayer was granted on the same day. The census of 1724 confirms the statement that Foltz had made only seven barrels of rice that year, and adds that he was sick the whole summer.

When the arduous work of clearing the land was done, the tilling of the soil began. With plow? Oh no! The company des Indes did not furnish plows. But why do we speak of plows? There were no horses nor oxen to draw them. The census of 1731 shows that, ten years after the arrival of the Germans, there was not yet a single horse on the whole German Coast; and the census of 1724 proves that, out of fifty-six German families enumerated, only seven had been given a cow each.

It is true there were 262 horses in 1731 outside of New Orleans, and the Tunica Indians also had thirty; but the 262 horses had been given by the company only to large planters, and the Indians had obtained theirs from the Spaniards. There were no horses for the German small farmers. All that was done for them up to the year 1731 was to sell to them occasionally a negro, for whom they had to grant the company a mortgage on all their movable and immovable property.

No draught animals, no plows, no cows, no wagons to haul the products—everything had to be carried home as best one could. Perhaps the Compagnie des Indes gave the colonists some wheel barrows, but there is not to be found any mention even of them. The only agricultural implements furnished were pickaxe, hoe, and spade. Imagine people working with these in the hot sun, on the hard ground and with bodies racked with malarial fever!

And when the day's work in the field was done, there was no evening rest inviting them home; for now began the heavy work on the "pilon," the hand mill, or pounding trough, to crush the corn and rice for their scanty meals. No meat! Where should it be obtained? The killing of cows was a crime at that time (and there were so few to kill!) and the people working during the day in the fields to utter exhaustion could not go hunting for game, and had not the means to keep an Indian hunter as most of the large concessioners did.

Rice, corn, and beans,
Corn, beans, and rice,
Beans, rice, and corn

constituted their daily fare, and Mississippi water their drink. No chickens, not an egg! The company did not furnish chickens. A pig or two, that was all! Chickens were furnished only by Governor Bienville, and only to those on Bienville's own land immediately above the city of New Orleans, to raise poultry for the city and to pay part of their ground rent to Monsieur Bienville in capons.

One can not blame the French *engagés* for running away from such a miserable existence. There is in Louisiana a popular saying, which is occasionally heard from Creoles when they speak of work uncommonly hard:

"It takes German people to do that."

Such is the reputation these German pioneers made for themselves in Louisiana! Yes, it took German people! They stood their work manfully, and most of them lay down and died long before their time!

Troubles With the Indians.

The Indians, too, were a source of constant worry, especially so about the year 1729, when the great massacre of the French, and also of some Germans, occurred in Natchez. Posts of observation were then established along the German Coast on high trees on the river bank, and when the men went out in the fields, women with flint-lock firearms went up into the tops of the trees to keep a sharp lookout, and to warn the men by shots when Indians sneaked out of the swamps and approached the habitations.

In the war following the Natchez massacre, the people of the German Coast seem to have taken a very active and a very creditable part. Charlevoix (IV., 269) says:

"The habitants commanded by Messrs. D'Arensbourg and de Laye (the director of the Meure concession, the river front of which was occupied by Germans) did also very well. They were also inclined to do with good will all the work that they were ordered to do."

Even as late as 1747 and 1748 Indian raids and depredations are reported. Most of these attacks were made upon the villages on the left bank, by Indians who were incited, armed, and often led by English traders. It was for this reason that the small military post on the German Coast, a wooden enclosure with one gun "en barbette," was built on the left side of the river.

In consequence of such instigation by the English, on the 8th of April, 1747, a band of Chacta Indians under their chief Bonfouca made a raid on the left bank of the Mississippi. On this occasion one German was killed, his wife wounded, and their daughter, together with three negroes and two negritoes, carried off as prisoners. The German girl was sold by the Indians to English traders, who took her to Carolina, "where the English governor was very active in stirring up other Indian nations to invade the Colony of Louisiana."

Then many Germans, fearing that the whole Chacta nation was on the war path, fled to New Orleans, and in order to induce them to return to their homes, soldiers had to be sent with them for their protection. When these, later, were withdrawn, the Germans crossed over to the right bank of the Mississippi where their principal establishments were, and "abandoned their houses and their well cultivated fields to the enemy and to the discretion of their animals." Thus governor Vaudreuil wrote on November 9th, 1748.

Another raid took place on November 9th, 1748. Indians appeared on the left bank "aux Allemands," on the habitation of one "Chuave" (Schwab) who had recently died. They found two Frenchmen there, Boucherau and Rousseau, and two negroes. All these were killed with the exception of a negro, who, having received only flesh wounds, jumped into the Mississippi to swim to the other side, assistance reaching him from the other bank when he was in the middle of the stream. Meanwhile the Indians, finding no further resistance, began to plunder. In their savaging they also seriously wounded a French dancing master by the name of Baby, who, on one of his regular tours of instruction, came riding along on a mule, which was too miserable to save his master by running away from the savages.[21]

The wounded negro, according to negro fashion, gave a very exaggerated account as to the number of Indians from which he had escaped, and so the German militia of the right bank was called out by D'Arensbourg; but there being no means of transportation to get the men across the Mississippi in sufficient numbers to cope with the enemies, reported to be so numerous, and the people fearing that, in the absence of the militia, the savages might cross the Mississippi and begin a massacre among the unprotected women and children on the right side of the river, the militia was kept back and divided into three troops to protect the upper, middle, and lower right coast. At the same time a messenger was sent down to New Orleans for troops to go up on the left bank and engage the Indians while the militia should prevent the savages from crossing over.

Instead of going to the aid of the Germans, however, Governor Vaudreuil went next day with twenty-two men to Bayou St. John, in the rear of New Orleans, to reinforce the soldiers already there and enable them to cut off the retreat of the Indians, in which purpose he succeeded to the extent of killing two savages. Governor Vaudreuil should not have been surprised, as he seems to have been, at D'Arensbourg's not crossing the Mississippi with his militia, for he, as governor, must have known that there were no transportation facilities, which it was his duty as governor to provide, especially after the raid of 1747 and previous ones, which always occurred on the left bank of the river.

In the nineteenth century, the relations between the Ger-

---

[21] "Baby taught the ladies the minuet and the stately bows with which they were to salute the governor and his wife." Fortier, I, 131.

mans and the Indians became very friendly. As late as 1845, thousands of Indians, following the migrating game, used to come from Illinois, Missouri, and Arkansas to Louisiana, to spend the winter in the south. They were given quarters in the outhouses of the farmers, and spent their time in hunting and making baskets. Like the migrating swallows, these Indians for generations visited at the same farms and became well acquainted with the white families, and much attached to them. On their arrival, the red men kissed the white children, and on returning from their hunting trips, they never failed to give them choice pieces of their booty. Their departure for the north was always a source of deep regret to the white boys, some of whom used to accompany the Indians on their hunting trips, and learned much about hunting from them.[22]

Better Times.

In spite of all the hardships which the pioneers had to endure and the difficulties to be encountered, German energy, industry, and perseverance conquered all; and although hundreds perished, the survivors wrested from the soil not only a bare living, but in course of time a high degree of prosperity also. Early travellers, who came down the Mississippi, describe the neat appearance of their little white houses, which stood in endless numbers on both banks of the Mississippi; and they also tell how these thrifty Germans used to row down to New Orleans in their boats with an abundance of their produce: vegetables, corn, rice, and later also indigo, to sell their goods on Sunday mornings in front of the cathedral; and how, at times, when non-producing New Orleans in vain waited for the provision ships from France or San Domingo, these German peasants more than once saved the city from heavy famine. Thus, in 1768, the provisions they furnished saved the Acadians.

Churches of the Germans.

In the Catholic church in New Orleans, on the site of the present St. Louis Cathedral, the first church in this part of the

---

[22] Communicated by Felix Leche, Esq., a Creole of German descent.

colony of Louisiana, the Germans of the German Coast first attended divine service; here they also had their children christened, here their weddings were celebrated. The cathedral records from 1720 to 1730 contain many German names.[23]

But in 1724, so the census of that year informs us, the Germans had already a chapel of their own on the German Coast, which then may have stood already for one or two years, as the river settlement was made in the late fall of 1721. This chapel was built on the right bank of the Mississippi, on the place now called "Le Sassier" (Trinity Plantation), below Bonnet Carré Bend in St. Charles parish.[24] It is interesting to note this fact and to remember that this chapel was built about the same time when the Jesuit Charlevoix reported (1722) that the people of New Orleans had "lent the Lord half of a miserable store for divine service and that they want the Lord to move out again and accept shelter in a tent." Visiting priests from New Orleans held divine service on the German Coast until a resident priest was appointed. In the colonial budget for 1729 (earlier budgets are not available) provision was made for such a one. He was Pater Philip, a Capuchin.

According to a map of the year 1731 (Crown Maps), the German settlement of that time began on the upper side of Bonnet Carré Bend, about four miles below Edgard, in St. John the Baptist parish, and extended from there down the Mississippi. But the map fails to show the German settlement on the other side of the river, where the census of 1724 places a number of Germans.

The first chapel, according to tradition, was replaced in 1740 by the first "Red Church" on the other side of the river, twenty-five miles above New Orleans.

The first Red Church was burned in 1806, and in the same year replaced by the second, the present Red Church. An irreparable loss was sustained here when, in 1877, a demented negro set fire to the priest's house, and all records of the church were burned. The rectory of the Red Church was not rebuilt. A

[23] See the author's *Geschichte der deutschen Kirchengemeinden im Staate Louisiana*, pages 11 to 17.

[24] Louisiana is the only state in the Union in which the word "parish" is used to designate a "county."

new parish was erected on the other side of the river, the Holy
Rosary Church, where the parish priest of Red Church now
resides.

CHURCH OF ST. CHARLES BORROMAEUS.
"RED CHURCH."

The name "Red Church" is due to the traditional coat of
red paint which both of these churches had and which made
them a landmark for the boats on the Mississippi River. Nearby
is the oldest existing cemetery of the Germans, with many beautiful tombs. One of them, that of the Rixner (originally "Richner") family, is said to have cost ten thousand dollars. The
tradition of the Rixner family about this tomb is that Geo. Rixner, who in 1839 married Amélie Perret, had, in order to please
his wife, to whom he was greatly devoted, laid aside ten thousand dollars to build a fine residence on his plantation. Before
this could be done, the good wife died, and the sorrowing husband built his wife a magnificent tomb with this money. George
Rixner never married again. His only child Amélie married
an Italian, Count de Sarsana. She died in Marsala, Italy, and
left a son, Ignatio.

In 1771, the Germans of the upper German Coast built the church of St. John the Baptist, in Edgard, upon the right side of the river, a few miles from the place where the first chapel had been. Fortunately, the records of this church have been preserved, and are in good condition. To that church the author paid more than thirty visits, and there he gathered rich material for his work.

CHURCH OF ST. JOHN THE BAPTIST.

The corner stone of the present church of St. John the Baptist was laid on the 4th of June, 1820, and it was consecrated on the 17th of March, 1822. It took the place of the first St. John the Baptist Church, erected about 1771. The records of the church begin in the year 1772 with the entry of the marriage of Anton Manz (now "Montz"), of the diocese of Strassburg, the son of Jos. M. and Anna Maria Laufer, who married Sibylla Bischof, daughter of Joseph Bischof and Anna Maria Raeser, of St. John. The Raeser family came to Louisiana in 1721.

On account of the dampness of the ground, the dead are

buried here in tombs above ground, and some very fine tombs belonging to the old colonial German families may be seen in this cemetery. About 1864, the portion of this parish on the opposite bank of the Mississippi was organized as the independent parish of St. Peter. The station "Reserve" of the Yazoo & Mississippi Valley Railway, thirty-five miles above New Orleans, is about half a mile from this church.

When, in 1769, the first church and cemetery of St. John were planned, there was some trouble to find the necessary ground for them. The Spanish General O'Reilly, hearing that some old bachelor had more land, twelve arpents, than he could attend to ordered him to furnish the necessary ground for both church and cemetery. To compensate him for his loss, the community was commanded to clear for him the same number of arpents on the remaining land of the man, and to give him the same number of new pickets as he had lost with the church land. This order was signed on the 21st of February, 1770. The original is still to be seen in the court house at Edgard.

Situation: The church of St. John the Baptist is immediately behind the levee, St. John the Baptist parish, Louisiana, two miles from St. John station of the Texas & Pacific Railway, thirty-five miles by rail above New Orleans. The post office on the place is called "Edgard."

The first parish priest (1772) was Pater Bernhard von Limbach, a German Capuchin, who later was transferred to St. Louis, Missouri.

The Census of 1721.

The Louisiana Historical Society received from Paris, in December, 1904, a copy of the census taken by M. Diron, Inspector General of the French troops in Louisiana and signed by him, Bienville, Le Blond de la Tour, Duvergier, and de Cormes, on the 24th of November, 1721.

If this were a complete census of Louisiana, we would have an accurate description of the state of affairs on John Law's concession on the Arkansas River at the time when the German Law people were there; and also an accurate account of the two old German villages on the German Coast, which were flooded by the great hurricane of 1721. Unfortunately, however, it covers only New Orleans and vicinity, from below English Turn to Cannes Brûlées.[25]

As a matter of general interest, it may be stated from this census that the white population of New Orleans in 1721 consisted of:

72 civilians, of whom 40 were married and had 29 children,	
44 soldiers, " " 14 " " " " no "	
11 officers, " " 2 " " " " one child each,	
22 ship captains and sailors, 9 " " " " 7 children,	
28 European laborers (*engagés*)	The names of the *engagés* are never given, neither is it stated whether or not they were married. The church records show that some of them were married.

There were also:
177 negro slaves,
21 Indian slaves,
36 cows, and
9 horses.

Only *nine* horses in the whole town! Not even the governor of the colony of Louisiana could boast of a horse, and the cannon and the ammunition for the troops must have been drawn either by the soldiers themselves, or by negroes or cows, for the nine horses were private property. Trudeau had four of them, and Pierre and Mathurin Dreux owned the other five.

Furthermore, in eleven years, from 1721 to 1732, the number of horses increased only *from nine to fourteen!* Dr. Manade, of Chartres street, had two horses in 1732; the butcher Caron, of Chartres street, owned one; the blacksmith Botson, the interpreter Duparc, and the concessioner Bruslées, all of St. Anne street, had one each; Dr. Alexander, of the hospital, owned one; clerk of the court Rossard, of Toulouse street, had three; and M. Marbaud, of Bourbon street, had four.

Judging from the family names the whole population of New Orleans was French in 1721, but there lived also one Ger-

---

[25] Cannes Brûlées was on the left bank of the Mississippi, six lieues or eighteen miles (by river) above New Orleans and immediately below the German Coast.

man family in New Orleans: "Johann Gustav Freitag, wife and child".

The town limits of New Orleans were then the river front, Dauphine, Ursuline and Bienville streets. At a later time "Chapitoulas Gate" was built at the upper end of the town, out of which ran the only road leading along the river up the coast, the "Chapitoulas Road".

All the land from the upper side of Bienville street up to the present "Southport", above Carrollton (Nine Mile Point), and from the Mississippi back to the present Claiborne avenue—213 1/2 arpents river front—belonged to Governor Bienville, who, after selecting the site for the future city of New Orleans in 1718, hastened to lay hold of as much as possible of the best land, adjacent to the coming city, and caused [26] the Superior Council of Louisiana to grant him this land immediately above New Orleans, as a concession, and to give him also a second concession of 112 arpents front on the other side of the Mississippi, beginning below the point of Algiers, "Pointe Saint Antoine", near the present Vallette street, and extending down the Mississippi.

After these two grants had been made by the Superior Council of Louisiana, on the 27th of March, 1719,[27] and while the matter was still pending before the directors of the Compagnie des Indes in Paris for their approval, a royal edict was issued on the 7th of November, 1719,[28] forbidding governors, lieutenant-governors, and intendants (Hubert, the intendant, had a fine concession in Natchez and another opposite New Orleans) to own plantations. They were allowed to have "vegetable gardens" only.

Notwithstanding this royal edict, Bienville, who had already received Horn Island in socage tenure,[29] had these two immense new grants approved by the directors in Paris on February 6th, 1720.[30]

---

[26] That Bienville himself demanded these grants from the company is shown by the wording of the official documents. "Sur la demande de Monsieur de Bienville," and again: "le terrain que vous avez choisy." Pages 12 and 20, *Concessions*, New Transcripts of the La. Hist. Soc.

[27] Volume *Concessions*, page 18.

[28] Fortier's *History of Louisiana*, I, 83.

[29] Grace King's *Bienville*, page 238.

[30] Volume *Concessions*, page 18.

In order to obey the letter, if not the spirit, of the royal edict, Bienville now designated 53 1/2 out of 213 1/2 arpents immediately above New Orleans as his habitation, "the vegetable garden", which extended from Bienville street to near our Felicity Road, and from the Mississippi to our Claiborne avenue— a pretty good sized "vegetable garden"—comprising more than the whole first district of the present city of New Orleans.

Not satisfied with this, Bienville made a second "vegetable garden" by taking forty-nine arpents front by a depth of eighty arpents of his grant on the other side of the river and designating this also as his habitation.[31]

And as he was not allowed to work the remainder of his two big grants as plantations, he conceived the plan of introducing into Louisiana a system of feudal tenure, selling these lands to people for very burdensome annual ground rent in money and products, and also in manual labor.

Some of Bienville's first victims were twelve German families, storm victims, whom he placed on his lands above "the vegetable garden" above New Orleans, about January 1st, 1723, but who soon tired of enjoying the benevolent arrangements of "The Father of the Colony", and left for other parts of Louisiana.[32]

On Bienville's land between Bienville street and Southport only one family lived in 1721. This was M. de Baume, attorney general of the colony at the time when the two grants were made to Bienville. He had six arpents front beyond the upper limit of "the vegetable garden", where he resided with his wife and two children. He had three *engagés*, nine negro slaves, five cows, and two horses.

In 1722 Bienville came to New Orleans and established himself on his land where he occupied the square bounded by Bienville, Iberville, Decatur and Chartres streets.[33] The square behind, bounded by Bienville, Iberville, Chartres and Royal streets, he sold, together with other lands, in 1726, to the Jesuit

---

[31] Volume *Concessions*, page 448. The people settled by Bienville on his Algiers' grant were all Canadians. Among them were three by the name of "Langlois."

[32] They went up to the German Coast.

[33] In a map of 1728 (see U. S. Census of 1880) this square is marked: "Terre concédée à Mr. de Bienville," and the square behind as: "Terrain aux Jesuites."

fathers, who, on the first of May, 1728, purchased another five arpents from him and gradually acquired the whole territory up to Felicity Road. The original Jesuits' plantation therefore began on Bienville street and not on Common street, as the legend says. Common street may have been the lower boundary at a later time, when it became necessary to use the ground from Bienville street to Canal street for the purpose of fortifying the town. This was after 1729, after the great massacre in Fort Rosalie.

Where Southport now stands, in the center of the great bend of the Mississippi above Carrollton, began "le village des Chapitoulas". Hence "Chapitoulas Gate" in New Orleans, "Chapitoulas Road" and our present "Tchoupitoulas street".

In Chapitoulas were the great plantations of Deubreuol, Chauvin de Léry, Chauvin la Frénière, and Chauvin Beaulieu, all Canadians. There was also, away from the river front, and two miles below Cannes Brûlées (Kenner), the so-called "Koly" concession. According to the census of 1721, there were on this place sixty-two white men, twelve white women with five children, forty-four negro slaves, two Indian slaves, five head of cattle, and four horses. The census says that on this place six hundred quarts of rice were made from fourteen quarts of seed rice.

There was a second so-called "Koly" plantation in Louisiana in 1721, called St. Catharine plantation, originally Hubert's concession, on which were, in 1723, forty-three white men, six white women with two children, forty-five negro slaves, two Indian slaves, fifty-two head of cattle, and two horses. These were, evidently, part of the same people who were moved to St. Catherine when the first "Koly" plantation was abandoned.

The "Koly" estate also owned a large house in New Orleans, on Chartres street, in which six Ursuline nuns lived with six boarding scholars and twenty-eight orphan girls. This house was later bought for a hospital, a sailor named Jean Louis having left a legacy of 10,000 livres for that purpose. This was the beginning of the "Charity Hospital" of New Orleans.

KOLY.

All Louisiana historians merely refer to Koly as a Swiss. This is all they say about him. But in a volume of the New

Transcripts of the Louisiana Historical Society the author found information which throws more light upon him. This volume contains a large number of official documents relating to the "Concession St. Catherine"; and in these papers, which do not state that Koly was a Swiss, "Jean Daniel Koly" is called "Councilor of the Financial Council of His Highness the Elector of Bavaria" (Elector Max Emanuel, who ruled from 1679 to 1726).

It appears from these documents that in 1718 an association was formed in Paris, of which Koly and the banker Deucher of Paris seem to have been the leading spirits. Among its members wère several French officials of high rank, and also "Jean Le Chambrier escuyer Envoyé de Sa Majesté le Roy de Prusse à la Cour de France." The association had a capital of 400,000 livres, and, on the 11th of December, 1719, received from the Compagnie des Indes a land concession in Louisiana of four leagues square, the location of which was to be decided by the association.

On the 29th of December, 1719, Koly and Deucher, in the name of their associates, entered into a contract with Faucon Dumanoir, engaging him for a term of eight years as the director general of the association, with instructions to proceed with the necessary number of officials and *engagés* to Louisiana and there to select and manage the lands of the association. The principal plantation was to be called "St. Catherine," smaller posts to be named by the director general.

Dumanoir embarked on the 28th of May, 1720, on board the ship St. André at L'Orient, and arrived in Biloxi on the 24th of the following August with eleven officers, 186 workmen, twenty-three women, and six children. According to the names on the passenger list, only a few Germans seem to have been among them: Jean Bierzel and Jean Mayeur. Among the French workmen of this concession was François Forestier of St. Malo, a locksmith (serrurier) who later became "armurier," *i. e.,* keeper of the armory of the king. François Forestier was the progenitor of the "Fortier" family in Louisiana.

In a letter dated Natchez, July 18th, 1721, Dumanoir describes his experiences on the voyage and in Biloxi. The Compagnie des Indes had engaged itself to transport *gratis* to Louisiana the men and belongings of the association, and to feed officers and men, the first named at the captain's table and the latter with sailors' rations, not only during the sea voyage but also until they should arrive at their concession. The food furnished on board was of such bad quality, that Dumanoir had to give his people of his own provisions, which he had taken with him for his concession to bridge over the time until the first crop could be made on the new concession; and, finally the company took forcibly from him more than four months' provisions and twenty-eight out of thirty-one large casks of wine. "This is the cause," Dumanoir complains in his letter, "why I have not drunk any wine for the last three months."

In Biloxi he found no sheds to store his goods, nor a hospital, and not even medicines for his sick. Ninety of his people died there of the fever which raged in Biloxi "for four years." There were no boats to take his men to the Mississippi, and they had to stay nearly eight months on the sandy shore. He himself built two barges in which he set off on the 23rd of April, 1721, with part of his men with whom he reached Natchez about the end of June. The rest of his people had to remain behind. Another authority says that they stayed in Biloxi for a whole year.

Dumanoir then had hardly enough provisions left to last for two months, which, together with the great loss of time, made it impossible for him to go into the wilderness and select a site for the new plantation. So Dumanoir, in January, 1721, bought Hubert's plantation in Natchez for 50,000 livres, and also twelve cows and two negroes from M. Raquet for 6,500 livres.

This was the best he could do under the circumstances, but his right to select four leagues square as a concession for his association was lost. Hubert's place offered many advantages. At Natchez there was a military post to furnish protection against the Indians, and there were already 160 arpents cleared which saved fifteen months of time, work, salaries, and other expenses. Moreover, the seed was in the ground for a large crop of provisions and tobacco. To satisfy immediate wants, however,

Dumanoir purchased another place, a little concession, the same mentioned under "Chapitoulas" in the census of 1721, which was later abandoned.

In 1727 charges of maladministration were made against Dumanoir, and he was deposed. It must have been then that Koly determined to come to Louisiana himself to take charge of the enterprise. He and his son were killed by the Natchez Indians in St. Catharine in the great massacre in 1729.

CONTINUATION OF THE CENSUS OF 1721.

The upper part of Chapitoulas was later called "La Providence," and extended to Cannes Brûlées, where M. Diron, the inspector general, had his concession. At this point the census of 1721 stops.

Seven lieues below New Orleans is English Turn. Immediately below this was at that time the second concession, the principal one being on the Yazoo River, of M. le Blanc, the French minister of war, and adjoining this was John Law's second concession, his principal one being on the Arkansas River. On this, the lower concession of Law, were, in 1721, five men, eleven women, fourteen children, and forty *engagés*. We have learned that all the Law people were Germans, and so we have a settlement of seventy Germans, in 1721, below English Turn.

This is all the information concerning the early Germans contained in the official census of 1721.

REMARKS AND OBSERVATIONS ON LOUISIANA.

There are some fifteen pages of "Remarks and Observations on Louisiana," probably written by some reviewing official, attached to the census of 1721. These "R. & O.," as they will be indicated hereafter, bear no signature, nor is the first part, referring to lower Louisiana, dated. The second part, dealing with the Illinois district, is dated "in March, 1722." The second part was, therefore, written much later than the official census report; and the first part, too, can not have been written earlier than February, 1722, because it mentions the exodus of the Germans from the Arkansas River as an historical event, although it did not take place earlier than February, 1722.

Of the Germans on the German Coast "R. & O." say that
"they may be composed of about 330 persons of both sexes and
of all ages."

We are also told that there were then still eighty German
people left on the Arkansas River. As La Harpe found only
forty-seven Germans there on his arrival, on the 20th of March,
1722, "R. & O." must have been written after the removal of
the people from there had begun and before it was completed.

"R. & O." and the Census Reports.

February, 1722, "R. & O." Estimate of population of German Coast, 330 persons.

May 15th, 1722, Official census of German Coast:

Karlstein = D'Arensbourg and an orphan boy...... 2 persons,
Mariental = 26 men, 30 women, 26 children......... 82 persons,
Hoffen   = 25 men, 29 women, 49 children.........103 persons,
Augsburg = 17 men, 20 women, 33 children......... 70 persons.

69 men, 79 women, 109 children.........257 persons.

The census of 1722, which is really a continuation of that
of 1721, covers the territory from Cannes Brûlées to the village
of the Tounicas, and the whole right bank besides. On the
right bank, two lieues above New Orleans, at a place called "Le
Petit Desert" (near Westwego) three German families are mentioned: three men, three women and seven children, who are not
included here as residents of the German Coast.

November, 1724. Official census:

German Coast—53 men, 57 women, 59 children, in all 169
persons.

1731. Official Census:

German Coast—42 men, 44 women, 88 children, in all 174
persons.

There is a great discrepancy between the figures of the
writer of "R. & O." and those of the census of 1722, although
there were scarcely three months time between them:

330 given by "R. & O.," against 257 enumerated in the
census.

Although the mortality among these Germans was very great, as we can see by comparing the official data of the different years enumerated above, this alone would not explain the difference between the estimate of "R. & O." and that of the census of 1722. There must have been some other cause.

And there was. There was an exodus, of which the official census of 1722, enumerating only those actually present on the day of enumeration, did not take notice, but which is mentioned in other official documents.

On the first of December, 1722, Governor Bienville wrote to the Superior Council that he intended to place from twelve to fifteen German families upon his land between New Orleans and Chapitoulas, and he specifies:

"Of those Germans who lost their subsistance by the great hurricane and are now compelled to seek employment in order to provide for their families".

He would not enter into contracts with them, however, without the consent of the Superior Council. Ten days afterwards the council approved these contracts

"With the Germans who have engaged themselves to begin a new establishment on account of the bad situation and the difficulties they encountered on the lands which they occupied 'aux Tensas' ".

"Le village des Tensas"[34] was part of the German Coast, known as the concession of M. De Meure. This De Meure, in 1721, sold the whole river front of his grant (four lieues square) to La Harpe, leaving a passage of only three arpents from the river front to the land in the rear, which latter he retained. The front lands were then taken up by the Germans.[35]

This correspondence between Bienville and the Superior Council proves that there was an exodus, and also establishes the fact that a number of Germans, who had been *habitants* were

---

[34] The Tensas Indians were removed, in 1714, to Mobile County, because the Oumas constantly and habitually waged a relentless war against them.

[35] As La Harpe also appears in March, 1722, on the Arkansas river, deposing Levens, the agent of John Law, taking the inventory, and placing Dudemaine Dufresne in charge, he seems to have acted in these transactions under the authority of the Compagnie des Indes.

compelled to become *engagés*. It also explains the apparent discrepancy between the estimate of "R. & O." and the census of 1722. The writer of "R. & O." did not know that so many storm victims had left their places to become *engagés,* and the census enumerator took cognizance only of those present on the day of enumeration.

The great mortality mentioned before appears when the census reports for 1722 and 1724 are compared. In these two years the number of the men decreased from 69 to 53, the women from 79 to 57, and the children from 108 to 59. Then came a change. The adults, not being reinforced by new immigration, continued to decrease in numbers, while the number of children born in the colony rose from 59 to 88, more than making up for the loss of grown people. We may well assume that from that year on the population of the German Coast continued to increase.

In connection with the census of 1731 an important fact must be mentioned. The large concessions granted in former years in Louisiana had not proved advantageous to the colony. Many concessioners did not come to Louisiana at all, holding their grants only for speculation. Others had not the means to improve them, and still others abandoned them after experimenting on the ground with insufficient capital, and experiencing all kinds of difficulties, and because of the unwise administration of the colony. So the Superior Council petitioned the king to cancel all concessions between Manchac and the gulf, in order that a readjustment could be had.

This cancellation was done by an edict issued on the 10th of August, 1728; and even Bienville, who in the preceding year had sold to the Jesuits some of his land above New Orleans, lost his concessions, although in his brief of remonstrance he cited the placing of twelve German families on that land as an evidence that he had tried to improve it.

Many lands, especially on the left bank of the Mississippi, opposite the German villages, were now open to *bona fide* settlers, and many changes in the occupants of the land occurred. Ambros Heidel, the progenitor of all the "Haydel" families in Louisiana, crossed the Mississippi and settled on the left bank. So did his old neighbor Caspar Dubs, the progenitor of all the "Toups" families, and so did Nikolaus Wichner, the progenitor of the "Vicners," "Vicnaires," and "Vickners," while all those German families who had settled on Bienville's lands between New Orleans and Chapitoulas, the storm victims, also went further up the river to live among their compatriots.

NAMES OF GERMAN HABITANTS ON BOTH BANKS OF THE MISSISSIPPI ABOVE NEW ORLEANS.

Official Census of 1724.

The official census taken in November, 1724, must always be the principal source of information concerning the founders of the German Coast in Louisiana. It will, therefore, be treated here at some length; and such notes will be added to it as were taken from other census reports, from church registers, and other official sources.

The official census of 1724 embraces the concessions and habitations on both sides of the Mississippi River from New Orleans to and including the German Coast. It consists of two parts of sixty entries each. The first part covers the right bank from the upper limits of the German villages (upper side of Bonnet Carré bend) down to a point nearly opposite New Orleans; and the second part begins at the upper town limit of New Orleans on the left bank (at what is now Bienville street) and follows the left bank up the river to a point ten lieues above and opposite the German villages, where the first part began.

Concerning the spelling of the German family names the reader is referred to the section of this work on the changes German names suffered at the hands of the French officials. Having met these names in many official records and church registers, and having found the same names spelt differently by many officials, and having also found original signatures of the German people, the author was in many instances able to restore the original German names. Where this was not possible, a question mark follows the name here.

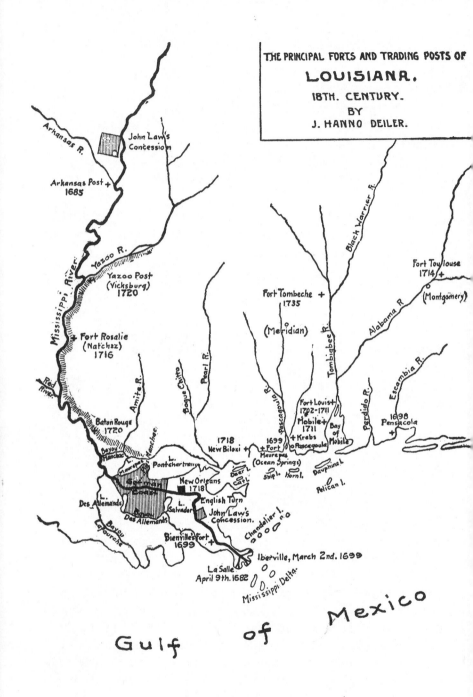

THE PRINCIPAL FORTS AND TRADING POSTS OF
LOUISIANA.
18TH. CENTURY.
BY
J. HANNO DEILER.

Gulf of Mexico

As to the names of the birthplaces, also, a few words of explanation are needed. As the German people pronounced these names usually in their home dialect, the French officials were entirely at sea as to their correct forms, and wrote them down so that, in many cases, they cannot be recognized. Many people also came from little hamlets the names of which are not to be found even in such works as Neumann's "Orts- und Verkehrs-Lexikon," which contains 75,000 names of places in the German empire, and gives the names of all places of 300 and more inhabitants.

Of frequent occurrence in this census, and of special importance, are the names "Palatinate" (Pfalz), "Mayence" (Mainz), and "Spire" (Speyer). The Palatinate of the eighteenth century was much larger than the present Palatinate. It included the northern portions of Baden and Wurtemberg, extending nearly to the towns of Heilbronn and Wimpfen, and the Elector Palatinate resided then in Heidelberg. Accordingly, some places given in this census as belonging to the Palatinate may now have to be looked for in Baden and Wurtemberg.

The name "Spire" may signify the city of Spire and the small territory that belonged to the bishop of Spire. But if Spire means the diocese of Spire, then the whole Palatinate is included. The bishop of Spire at that time resided alternately in Spire and Durlach.

The name "Mayence" may mean the city of Mayence; it may mean the electorate of Mayence, a much larger territory, and it may mean the archdiocese of Mayence. The last included, also, the whole of Franconia, with the dioceses of Wuerzburg and Bamberg, which now belong to Bavaria.

Of the names of the three German villages, "Hoffen," "Mariental," and "Augsburg," on the German Coast of Louisiana, and mentioned in the census of 1724, two, Hoffen and Augsburg, occurred before in the passenger lists of the four pest ships which sailed from L'Orient, in France, on the twenty-fourth of January, 1721. They were used in the passenger lists to indicate the parish of birth of some of the emigrants.

RIGHT BANK OF THE MISSISSIPPI.

The German Village of Hoffen, 10 Lieues Above New Orleans. November 12th, 1724.

Simon Lambert is mentioned as "premier habitant et le plus haut sur le fleuve," the habitant living highest up on the right bank of the Mississippi. This location was on the upper side of Bonnet Carré Bend, about four miles below Edgard in the parish of St. John the Baptist. Lambert's habitation bears the number one. Thence the census enumerator proceeded down the right side of the river.

1. *Simon Lambert,* of Oberebesheim, diocese of Spire, Catholic; 40 years of age. His wife; and a son, 18 years of age. Five arpents cleared. Gave up his first place on account of inundation.

   1726: Six arpents cleared.
   1731: Occupant of this place, Jean Martin Lambert, son of the aforementioned, with wife and child.
   1764: Bartholomew Lambert, son of Jean Martin Lambert and Anna Eve Lambert, married Margarethe Troxler, daughter of Geo. T. and Marie Agnes Troxler.

2. *Conrad Friedrich,* of Rothenberg, diocese of Spire. (There is one Rothenberg east of Mannheim.) Catholic; 50 years old. His wife and three children. A daughter of 18 years; the youngest child five years old. Gave up first place on account of inundation. "A good worker".

   1726: Six arpents cleared.
   1726: Daughter Anna Barbara married Friedrich Merkel from Wurtemberg, and, after whose death she married Nikolaus Wichner. Nikolaus Wichner and Anna Barbara Friedrich were the progenitors of most of the "Vicners", "Vicnaires" and "Vickners".
   1728: Daughter Anna Maria married Edw. Poupart, of Paris.
   1731: One child at home. Two negroes; one cow.
   About 1750 Sebastian Friedrich, son of Conrad Friedrich, married Regina Heidel (Haydel), daughter of Ambros Heidel, of St. John the Baptist. They lived below New Orleans.

3. *Johann Georg Troxler,* of Lichtenberg in Alsace. Catholic; 26 years old. A mason. His wife. "Fort bon travailleur". Two and one-half arpents cleared, on which he has been only since the beginning of the year having left the village in the rear.

Exposed to inundation. Absent because of bad health. His wife is also sick. Lost his crop and his house. A neighbor, who cooked in a shed attached to Troxler's house, accidentally set fire to it.
> 1731: Two children. Two negroes; one cow.
> Johann Georg Troxler was the progenitor of all the "Troxler" and "Trosclair" families in Louisiana.

4. *Johann Georg Bock,* from the neighborhood of Fort Kehl in Baden. Catholic; 38 years old; weaver. His wife with child at the breast. One and a half arpents cleared. Two years on the place.
> 1729: Marie Francoise, daughter of J. G. Bock and Cath. Hislinger, baptized.
> 1731: Three children. One negro.

Now come the two tracts of land abandoned by Lambert and Friedrich.

5. *Wilhelm Ziriac,* also "Querjac", "Siriaque", and "Siriac", of Ilmenstadt, near Mayence. Formerly coachman to King Stanislaus. Catholic; 50 years old. His wife and daughter, seven years old. Two and a half arpents cleared. Two years on the place. "One of the more well to do people of the community. A good worker."
> 1731: Only husband and wife mentioned. His daughter became the first wife of Ludwig Wiltz, the progenitor of the New Orleans branch of the Wiltz family, which is now extinct in the male line. All of the name of Wiltz now living belong to the Mobile branch of the family.

6. *Johann Callander,* of 'Aubrequin (Ober . . . ?), Palatinate. Catholic; 26 years old. His wife. A daughter. Sister-in-law; mother-in-law. One year on the place. Six arpents cleared, two and a half of which he bought from Peter Schmitz, and two and a half of which belonged to his mother-in-law and his children.
> 1731: One child. One negro; one cow.

7. *Stephan Kistenmacher,* of Cologne. Catholic; 39 years old. His wife and a daughter of 10 years. One and a half arpents cleared. Two years on the place. "Sick, broken down, miserable."
> 1728: His daughter Margarethe married Louis Leonhard, from the Arkansas post.
> 1731: Husband, wife and child. One *engagé.* One negro; one cow.

8. *Jeremias Wagner*, of Orensburg (?) in the marquisate of Ansbach (Bavaria). Lutheran; 27 years of age. Hunter. His wife with a child at the breast. Sister-in-law. Two arpents cleared. One year on the place. "Very good man and a great hograiser". 1726: Six arpents cleared.

9. *Leonhard Magdolff*, of Hermnnse (?), Wurtemberg. Catholic; 45 years old. His wife. An adopted orphan boy, 10 years old. Two and a half arpents cleared. One year on the place. "A good worker. Has a very fine garden, is well lodged, and very prosperous in his affairs."
      1726: Six arpents cleared.
      1731: No children. Three cows.

10. *Andreas Schantz* (Chance), of Hochhausen, Franconia. Catholic; 25 years old. Miller. His wife with a child at the breast. Stepdaughter of 15 years. "A good man, well lodged." Has a cow from the company and a calf of .eight days. A big hog and two little pigs.
      1726: Andreas Schantz married Maria Magdalena Gaffel, daughter of Leonhard G. and Cath. Wolf.
      1731: Two children. Four negroes; four cows.

11. *Johann Georg Betz*, of Weibstadt, diocese of Spire. Catholic; 32 years old. Butcher and *prévôt*. His wife with a child at the breast. An orphan girl, nine years of age. Three arpents cleared. Three years on the place. A cow, a calf, and two pigs.
      1727: On the first of July, 1727, Betz, his wife, and two children are reported as inmates of the hospital in New Orleans, and on the 24th of August Betz died. His widow, who was a sister of Ambros Heidel (Haydel), then married Caspar Diehl of Alsace. The whole family, Diehl, his wife, two children, "a brother" (whose brother?) were murdered in 1729 by the Natchez Indians in the great massacre in Natchez.

12. *Johann Adam Matern*, of Rosenheim, in Upper Alsace. Catholic; 26 years old. Weaver. His wife with a child at the breast; two sisters-in-law, 18 and 20 years of age. One and a half year on the place. Two and a half arpents cleared. "A good worker", who deserves some negroes. Three pigs.
      1731: Three children. Three negroes; seven cows.

13. *Caspar Dubs* (Toups) from the neighborhood of Zurich, Switzerland. Protestant; 40 years of age. Butcher and *prévôt*. His wife; two boys, 10 and 12 years old. Two years on the place. One and a half arpents cleared. Three pigs.
      1728: Caspar Dubs married Maria Barbara Kittler, from Wurtemberg.

1731: Six arpents cleared.
Caspar Dubs was the progenitor of all the Toups families in Louisiana.

14. *Ambros Heidel* (Haydel), of Neukirchen, electorate of Mayence. Catholic; 22 years old. Baker. His wife; his brother, 18 years old; his brother-in-law, aged 13, crippled. One and a half year on the place. "Good worker, very much at ease." One pig.
    Ambros Heidel's younger brother is mentioned for the last time in 1727. It is possible that he was murdered by the Natchez Indians with the family of his sister. See No. 11. From the entry there it does not appear whether the brother murdered was the husband's or the wife's brother.
    1731: Ambros Heidel, wife, two children. One *engagé*. Three negroes and two cows.

15. *Jacob Ritter,* of Lustuen in Wurtemberg (Lustnau near Tubingen?). Catholic; 28 years old. Shoemaker. His wife. One and a half arpents cleared. Six months on the place. One pig.
    1726: Four arpents cleared.
    1731: Two cows.

16. *Michael Vogel,* of Altdorf, Suevia, Germany. Catholic; 40 years old. Cooper. A little hard of hearing. Son of two years, daughter of eleven years in New Orleans. Sixteen verges cleared. (Ten verges=one arpent.) Two years on the place. One pig.
    1726: Four arpents cleared.
    1726: Margarethe Vogel, his daughter, married Jean Bossier, farmer from Natchitoches.
    1731: Two children. One negro; two cows.

17. *Sebastian Funck,* of Hagenau, Alsace. Catholic; 30 years old. His wife. Child of one year; orphan girl of 16 years. Two years on the place. Five arpents cleared, which he bought from two Germans, of whom one went to Natchitoches, while the other took land from Governor Bienville near New Orleans, which he has now held two years. One pig.
    1726: Husband, wife, two children. Four arpents cleared.

18. *Michael Horn,* of Limbal, near Mayence. Catholic; 39 years old. His wife and a daughter of eight years. Fifteen verges cleared. Fifteen days on the place. Came from "the old village". His sickness prevents him from succeeding. Michael Horn's daughter married Louis Toups.
    1726: Four arpents cleared.

19. A strip of land of eight verges for the surgeon of the community. A hut on it. Abandoned.

Here ends the village of Hoffen, and the census man now leaves the river front and proceeds to the two old villages in the rear, which were mentioned before. *Old German Village (i. e., the "second" one. See before.).* Three-fourths of a mile from the Mississippi.

20. *Balthasar Monthé,* of Troppau, in Silesia, Germany. Catholic; 42 years old. His wife. Daughter of 13 months. One and a fifth arpents cleared. Three years on the place. "A good worker. Everything well arranged on his place. Was sick the whole summer." Two pigs. He died in 1727.

21. *Johann Georg Raeser,* of Biebrich, in the electorate of Mayence. Catholic; 32 years old. Blacksmith. His wife. An orphan girl of 18 years. Two arpents cleared. Three years on the place. "Well arranged. Good worker."

    1726: Husband, wife, three children, brother-in-law. Six arpents cleared. One pig.

    1731: Husband, wife, one child.

22. *Johann Jacob Bebloquet* (?) of Lamberloch, Alsace. Lutheran; 36 years old. Hunter. His wife. Three children, two boys and one girl, ranging from two to thirteen years of age. One and a half arpents cleared. Three years on the place. Two pigs. "Well arranged. Good worker."

23. *Johann Cretzmann* (Kretzmann), of canton Berne, Switzerland. Calvinist; 46 years old. His wife; son of five years. One and a half arpents cleared. "His affairs well regulated. Demands his passage." Did not get it.

    1726: As widower of Barbara Hostmann, Johann Cretzmann married Susanna Rommel (Rome), daughter of Heinrich Rommel, and sister of Johann Rommel. See No. 26.

    1731: Husband; wife; three children. Six arpents cleared.

24. *Balthasar Marx,* of Wullenberg, Palatinate (one Wollenberg near Wimpfen), Catholic; 27 years old. Nailsmith. His wife, 22 years old. "His wife had a miscarriage last year on account of working at the pounding trough ('pilon'). He went to New Orleans to get some salt and had to give a barrel of shelled rice for three pounds. His affairs excellently arranged. Good worker." One and a half arpents cleared. Three years on the place.

    1731: Husband, wife, two children. One *engagé.* One negro; three cows.

    1775: *Jean Simon Marx,* son of Balthasar and Marianne Aglae Marx, married Cath. Troxler, daughter of Nik. T. and Cath. Matern (St. James parish).

25 Bernard Wich, of Tainlach, in Wurtemberg. Lutheran; 46 years old. His wife. Three children, a boy and two girls, from 13 years down to two months. Two arpents cleared. A pig.

    1731: Two children. One *engagé*. One negro.

26. *Johann Rommel* (now Rome), of Kinhart, Palatinate. Catholic; 24 years of age. Tailor. His wife. One and a half arpents cleared. Three years on the place. A pig.

    1728: Jean Rommel baptized.
    1731: Three children. Two cows.

27. *Catharine Weller* (ine), 49 years old, from Heilbronn, Wurtemberg, widow of August Paul, a Lutheran, a tailor. "Expects a child. Alone and poor. Has no provisions and needs some assistance. Six verges cleared."

28. *Anna Kuhn*, widow of Johann Adam Zweig (Labranche). Her husband was a Catholic, and died in Biloxi. Daughter of twelve years. One and a half arpents cleared. "Has no provisions and no seed for the next year. Needs some assistance."

    1729: Daughter Anna Margarethe Zweig married Pierre Bridel, a soldier, and a native of Bretagne. According to the marriage entry the bride was born in Bollweiler, Alsace.

29. *Magdalena Fromberger*, 50 years old. Catholic; widow of George Meyer from Ingitippil (?), Suevia, Germany. "Her son, Nik. Mayer, is crippled but industrious in the cooper trade. He also makes galoches which are a great help when shoes are scarce. An orphan girl, 20 years old. One and a half arpents cleared. Three years on the place. A pig.

    1731: Nik. Meyer. His wife and a child. One *engagé*. Two negroes; two cows.

30. *Margarethe Reynard* (Reinhard?), from Bauerbach, Baden. Catholic; 46 years old. Separated from Johann Leuck (?), who lives on the Mississippi. Daughter from first marriage, aged seven years. Seven verges cleared. Three years on the place.

31. *Catherine Hencke*, of Horenburg, Brandenburg, widow of Christian Grabert, a Catholic, who died in Biloxi, aged 50 years. A daughter, 14 years old. Both sick. She needs some assistance and is very willing to work. Two arpents cleared.

32. *Christian Grabert*, Grabert, of Brandenburg. Catholic; 23 years old. His wife. An orphan child, 13 years old. Two arpents cleared. Three years on the place. One pig.

    1726: Christian Grabert, his wife, mother-in-law, sister-in-law, and sister. Six arpents cleared.

1731: Husband, wife, three children. Two cows. Descendants of the Grabert family still live in Ascension parish, La.

33. *Andreas Necker,* of Dettenhausen, Wurtemberg. Lutheran; 36 years old. Miller. His wife. Two arpents cleared. One year on the place. Two pigs.

34. *Jacob Oberle,* of Zabern, Alsace. Catholic; 35 years old. Two arpents cleared. One year on the place.

The four arpents occupied by Necker and Oberle were situated between the two old villages and had served as a cemetery; but when the German people moved to the river front this cemetery was abandoned, whereupon Necker and Oberle took possession of it "a year ago". D'Arensbourg, however, whose land was contiguous to the cemetery, also claimed it on the ground that these four arpents had been cleared by the community.

("First") Old German Village.

One mile and a half from the Mississippi and adjoining the "second" village.

35. *Andreas Schenck,* from Saxony; Lutheran; 35 years old. Farmer, *prévôt* of a village. His wife and a child of two years. Land at discretion. Always serves with the troops as a musician.

1727: Andreas Schenck, wife and two children.

36. *Marcus Thiel,* of Bergwies, Silesia. Lutheran; 43 years old. Shoemaker. His wife. Land at discretion. Always sick.

37. *Moritz Kobler,* of Berne, Switzerland. Calvinist; 64 years old. Butcher. Served for thirty years in France in Swiss regiments. His wife. Land at discretion. Wants to return to France.

1729: Kobler's widow, Emerentia Lottermann, of Berne, married in this year Jacob Weisskraemer, from Bavaria, whose wife as well as his parents, Abraham and Magdalena W., had died at Fort Balize at the mouth of the Mississippi. In 1745 Jacob Weisskraemer married in Pointe Coupée Margarethe Françoice Sara, the widow of one Jolier.

38. *Karl Friedrich D'Arensbourg,* "captain reformé", aged 31 years. An orphan boy from 10 to 12 years old. A cow and a calf from the company. A bull belonging to him. Two pigs. Twelve arpents. Not much cleared from lack of force.

The census here informs us that the village just mentioned (the first old German village) had been founded by twenty-one German families, that some had died and others had moved to the river front, having been drowned out by the great hurricane three years previous. Schenck, Thiel and Kobler seem to have come over from the second village. This is the reason why these three had "land at their discretion," there being, as the census remarks, at least 100 arpents of beautifully cleared land in the neighborhood of this village, cleared, no doubt, by the twenty-one German families, the founders of the first village. But now, the census continues, these three men also want to leave and move to the other village (the second one), nearer to those abandoned lands, which they would now like to take up. This, the census man thinks, would be right as far as those lands are concerned which were abandoned more than a year ago, because the parties who left had in the meantime been able to clear enough new land to support their families and to continue farming. The fourteen families remaining in the second village, nearer the river, were all doing well, except the widows, and did not think of moving.

Having completed the two villages in the rear, the compiler of the census now evidently begins again at the river front, going down.

39. *Andreas Traeger* (now Tregre), of Donauwoerth, Bavaria. Catholic; 37 years old; hunter. His wife with a child at her breast. Three arpents cleared. Two years on the place. "A good worker. Well lodged. His yard, 90 x 90, staked off with palisades. Well cleared. Birds have caused a great deal of damage." One cow from the company. One pig.
    1726: Four arpents cleared.
    1731: Husband, wife, three children. Two negroes; three cows.
    Andreas Traeger was the progenitor of all the Tregre families in Louisiana.

40. *Jacob Lueck,* of Weissenburg. Forty-five years old. Separated from his wife, who lives in the village (See No. 30). "Left his place to go to Natchez, but is back now. Lazy, and a very bad man."

41. *Andreas Hofmann,* from the marquisate of Ansbach, Bavaria. Catholic; 27 years old. His wife. A daughter aged seven years. One and a half arpents cleared. A pig.
    1726: Four arpents cleared.
    1731: Husband, wife and four children.

4-. *Mathias Friedrich,* of Weilersheim, Alsace. (There were two Friedrich families in the colony then.) (See No. 2.) Catholic; 29 years old. His wife with a child at the breast. An orphan girl, aged 15 years. One and a half arpents cleared. "Good worker." A cow from the company. A calf and three pigs.
    1726: Husband, wife, and three children. Six arpents cleared.
    1731: Four cows.

43. *Bernhard Reusch,* from the Palatinate. Catholic; 52 years of age. Tailor. His wife. A son of fifteen and a daughter of eleven years. One and a half arpents cleared. Two years on the place. Water caused much damage. Two pigs.
    1726: Four arpents cleared.

44. *Paul Klomp* (Klump?), of Bauerbach, near Karlsruhe, Baden. Catholic; 30 years old. His wife. A son three and a half years old. An orphan boy of 12 years. One and a half arpents cleared. Three years on the place. Ground overflowed. Has been sick.
    1724: Four arpents cleared.

45. *The Chapel* with house and kitchen. Garden. Cemetery of about one and a half arpents. It was at the completion of this new cemetery that the cemetery between the two old villages was abandoned.

46. *Adam Schmitz,* a widower of Isnen, Suevia, Germany. Lutheran; 44 years old. Shoemaker. A daughter of nine years. Two years on the place. Eight verges cleared. "Works at his trade, making galoshes."

47. *Johann Rodler,* of Rastadt, Baden. Catholic; 35 years old. Locksmith. Works at his trade. His wife. Two years on the place. Eight verges cleared. Deaf.
    1726: Four arpents cleared.

48. *Anton Distelzweig,* of Selz, Alsace. Catholic; 29 years old. His wife. One child, one and a half years old. "Good worker." Three arpents or 32 verges cleared.

49. *William Pictot,* 50 years old, from Bretagne.

50. *Friedrich Merkel,* from Wurtemberg. Catholic; 30 years old. His wife Marianne Kohleisen. Sixteen verges cleared. Two years on the place. "Good worker." Two pigs.

1726: Four arpents cleared. In the same year Friedrich Merkel married Anna Barbara Friedrich, daughter of Conrad F. and Ursula Frey. (See No. 2). Merkel's name occurs for the last time in the census of 1727. Anna Barbara Friedrich, his widow, then married Nik. Wichner. (See No. 2).

51. *Peter Muench,* of Oberheim, in the Palatinate. Catholic; 40 years old. His wife. A son, one year old. Two arpents cleared. Two years on the place. Works at his trade.
1726: Four arpents cleared.

52. *Andreas Struempfl,* of Ottersheim, near Fort Kehl, Baden. Catholic; 23 years old. His wife. Two daughters. Two arpents cleared. Two years on the place. A cow and a calf; two pigs.
1728: Anna Barbara Struempfl baptized.
Another daughter by the name of Agnes married, about 1748, Johannes Ettler, of Colmar, Alsace.
1731: Three children. Two cows.

53. *Johann Adam Riehl,* of Hatzweiler, Basle, Switzerland. Catholic; 45 years old. Carpenter. His wife. Daughter of five months. One and a half arpents cleared. Two years on the place.

54. *Jacques Poché,* 45 years old, native of Omer, in Artois.

55. *Joseph Wagensbach* (now Waguespack), of Schwobsheim, Upper Alsace. Catholic; 23 years old. His wife. One and a half arpents cleared. Two years on the place.
1726: One child. Six arpents cleared.
1731: Three children. Two negroes; two cows.
Joseph Wagensbach was the progenitor of all the Waguespack families in Louisiana.

56. *Sibylla Heil,* widow of Wiedel, 37 years old, of Elchingen, Suevia, Germany. Catholic. Two years on the place. One and a half arpents cleared. "A good worker."

57. *Johann Adam Edelmeier,* of Reiheim, Palatinate. Calvinist; 50 years old. Cooper. Two boys, 10 and 14 years of age. A daughter, Maria Barbara, married Lionnois, a sailor from Lyons. Three arpents cleared. Two pigs. "A very good worker, who deserves attention."
1726: Six arpents cleared.
1728: Marie Christine Edelmeier baptized.
1731: Five children. One negro; two cows.

58. *Philipp Zahn,* of Grosshoeflein, Hungary. Catholic; 25 years of age. His wife. Three arpents cleared. Two years on the place. A pig.

1726: One child. Four arpents cleared.

1727: As widower of Margarethe Wiethen (ine) Philipp Zahn married in this year Marie Schlotterbecker of Wurtemberg, widow of Jacob Stalle and sister of the wife of Thomas Lesch.

The census at this time mentions the land forming the passage of three arpents' width, leading from the river front to the concession of M. de Meure. According to a map of 1731, this place was about two miles above Hahnville.

59. *Johann Jacob Foltz* (now "Folse"), of Ramstein, Palatinate. Catholic; 26 years old. Shoemaker. His wife. A child of one year. Four arpents cleared. Two years on the place. One pig. This year made only seven barrels of rice on account of inundation. Was sick the whole summer.

1731: Two children. Two cows.

60. *Bernhard Anton,* of Schweigen, in Wurtemberg. Lutheran; 30 years old. His wife. A boy, 10 years old. About four arpents cleared. Two pigs. Two years on the place. Made this year 20 barrels of rice, and would have also made 60 barrels of corn, if there had been no inundation. "Good worker."

1731: Three children. One *engagé.* Six cows.

After enumerating these families, the census of 1724 continues:

"All these German families enumerated in the present census raise large quantities of beans and mallows, and do much gardening, which adds to their provisions and enables them to fatten their animals, of which they raise many. They also work to build levees in front of their places.

"If all these small farmers were in the neighborhood of New Orleans they could raise vegetables and poultry. They could make their living well and add to the ornament of the town, as their small frontage on the river brings their houses with the gardens behind them so close together that they look like villages. But this agreeable condition unfortunately does not exist in New Orleans, owing to the greed for land of those who demanded large concessions, not with the intention of cultivating them, but only of reselling them.

"If these German families, the survivors of a great number who have been here, are not assisted by negroes, they will gradually perish; for what can a man and his wife accomplish on a piece of land, when, instead of resting themselves and taking their meals after their hard work, they must go to the pounding trough (*pilon*) to prepare their food, a very toilsome work, the consequences of which are dangerous for men and women. Many receive injuries, and many women get seriously hurt. When one of the two falls sick, it is absolutely necessary that the other should do all the work alone, and thus both perish, examples of which are not rare.

"The ground is so hard in the lower part of the colony that one must always have the hoe ready, and the weeds come out so strong and so quickly, that it seems after a short while as if no work had been done at all. The land is covered with dead trees and stumps, and these people have no draught animals (as this census shows there was not a single horse on the German Coast, and of the 56 families only six had cows), they cannot use the plow, but must always work with the pickaxe and the hoe.

"This together with the hard work on the *pilon*, causes these poor people to perish, who are good workers and willing, and who do not desire anything more than to remain in a country where they are free from burdensome taxation and from the rule of the master of their land—a lot quite different from that of the peasants in Germany.

"They would consider themselves very happy to get one or two negroes, according to the land they have, and we would soon find them to be good overseers. The only thing to be done would be to visit them once or twice a year, to see what use they are making of them, and to take the negroes away from the lazy ones and give them to the industrious. But this would hardly be necessary, as these people are by nature industrious and more contented than the French.

"They could also feed their negroes very well on account of the great quantities of vegetables they raise. They could also sell a great deal to the large planters, and these, assured of a regular supply, could give more attention to the raising of indigo, the cutting of timber, and to other things suitable for exportation to France and Cape Frances (San Domingo). I am persuaded that a great timber trade could be established with the West Indian Islands, where timber is getting scarcer and is dear."

LEFT BANK OF THE MISSISSIPPI RIVER.

Continuation of the Census of 1724.

The land immediately above New Orleans and on the same side of the Mississippi, beginning beyond the moat of the upper town limit (now foot of Bienville street), and extending up to the center of the great bend of the river at Southport, beyond Carrollton, belonged to M. Bienville—in all, 213½ arpents river front.

This is, no doubt, the land which the census enumerator, a French official, quoted above, had in view when he said, "If

these German farmers were in the neighborhood of New Orleans
* * * ." And when he speaks of "the greed of those who
demanded large concessions," he evidently referred also to Governor Bienville.

The lower portion of Bienville's land—from Bienville street
to somewhere about Felicity road, 58½ arpents' front—Bienville
reserved for his own habitation. Of this tract he sold a part
to the Jesuit fathers. From Felicity road up to Southport
he placed, as has been stated, twelve German and a few
French families, most of whom received their titles on and after
the first of January, 1723. But by the time the census of 1724
was taken, a number of these had left. The fact that the Germans had already once before lost their all by a great hurricane
and inundation, and the failure of Bienville to build a levee, although he had guaranteed one to them in their titles, and the
consequent inundations they were subjected to even in the first
year, together with the exacting conditions of rental to be ful-
filled—all these were causes to compel these people to sell
out their contracts as quickly as they could. Some had already
left during the first year, and Jacob Huber, the last German to
remain on Bienville's land, stayed only from 1723 to 1727.

Partly from census reports, and partly from chains of titles
of Bienville's hands, the author has been able to ascertain the
names of most of the German storm victims who settled on Bienville's lands:

Peter Bayer, from Wankenloch, near Durlach, Baden, who had
taken six arpents of Bienville's land above New Orleans.

Caspar Hegli, a Swiss, from near Lucerne. "Six arpents. Catholic;
35 years old. His wife. A daughter. Two orphan boys. A
cow, a heifer, a young bull, and three pigs. Two years on the
place. Used two and a half barrels of seed rice and did not make
more than three barrels on account of inundation. Has a very
fine garden enclosed by palisades. He has made a good levee
and is a good worker. He deserves a negro." (Census of
1724.)

Jacob Huber, with six arpents. "Native of Suevia, Germany.
Catholic; 45 years old. His wife, son of 16 years. One *engagé.* One cow, one heifer, a pig. Made no crop on account
of inundation. Good worker." (Census of 1724.)

Jacob Huber's son Christoph married Marie Josephine St. Ives. Descendants write the name now "Oubre", "Ouvre", "Hoover".

Andreas Krestmann, or Christmann, from Augsburg, with his two sons, 10 and 12 years old. Six arpents. "Wheelwright. His wife. Two orphan girls, eight and fifteen years old. Two years on the place. A cow, a heifer, a calf and three pigs. He is industrious and is at work fencing in his cleared land. He made a good levee and paid in advance the workmen who made it for him at a cost of 100 pistoles. Deserves a negro."

These four men occupied a portion of Bienville's land from the present First street of New Orleans to Napoleon avenue. Further up, beginning about the upper line of Audubon Park, were:

Simon Kuhn, of Weissenburg, Ansbach, Bavaria. "His wife, daughter, son-in-law, Daniel Hopf, 20 years of age of Cassen, diocese of Spire. Orphan boy, 12 years old. Cow, calf, three pigs. One year on the land. Had to change his engagements twice, having been forced to give up his cabin on account of water. Good worker." (Census of 1724.) An elder daughter of Simon Kuhn, Anna Kuhn, was the widow of Johann Adam Zweig (Labranche), who had died in Biloxi. She had a daughter of the age of 12 years. The orphan boy, 12 years old, was, no doubt a relative, and very likely that Jean Labranche who, in 1737, married Susanna Marchand and became the progenitor of all the Labranche families in Louisiana. Daniel Hopf (French spelling "Yopf" and "Poff") married, in 1727, Anna Maria Werich, of Lampaitz, German Lorraine. A daughter of this second marriage, Renée "Poff", married, 1752, in Pointe Coupée, Pierre Baron.

Thomas Lesch (now "Leche" and "Laiche"), with three arpents. "His wife. One *engagé.*" (Census of 1726.) Thomas Lesch married, in 1725, in the cathedral of New Orleans, Anna Schoderbecker of Wurtemberg. Only daughters were born from this marriage:

> *Margarethe Lesch* married one Peter Engel, a carpenter, whose name occurs also in the spelling "Aingle", "Ingle", "Hingle", and "Engle". There were three sons, Simon, Sylvestre and Santjago Hingle, who married into the Bura family in Plaquemines parish (Bura's Settlement). The "Hingle" family is quite numerous there.

> *Regina Lesch,* another daughter of Thomas Lesch, married one Christian Philippson.

Joseph Strantz, with three arpents.

One *Mueller,* with six arpents.

Johann Weber, the progenitor of the "Webre" families in Louisiana, with six arpents near the upper limits of Bienville's lands. now Carrollton. He was born near Fort Kehl, Baden, and was then 24 years old. (Census of 1724.) His wife was Marie Stadler, who came to Louisiana with her parents, Ulrich and Maria Stadler, on one of the four pest ships. "Mother-in-law, an orphan girl, aged 16 years. Cow, heifer, bull, four pigs. One year on the place."

The conditions under which these lands were given to the German storm victims by Bienville, were: From six to eight livres annual ground rent for each arpent and, every year, two capons and two days' work "in the form of *corvée*" for each arpent. Jacob Huber paid eight livres ground rent. Bienville subjected even the Jesuit fathers, who, on the first of May, 1728, bought five arpents from him, to conditions similar to these, including even that of *corvée.* This is true, also, of the Canadians who held lands from him on the Algiers side of the river.

The people of Bienville's lands must also repay the advances made to them by Bienville. These consisted usually of provisions for one year, a cow in calf, two hogs, four chickens with a cock, and the necessary utensils and agricultural implements. Utensils, provisions and implements must be paid for at the end of the first two years. The cow must be returned within three years, and of all the cattle raised in excess of the first twelve head Bienville was to receive one half. For the two hogs furnished he demanded a fat hog every second year, and for the four chickens and the cock six fat hens or capons were demanded every year.

In the census of 1726 these Germans were called "Vasseaux allemands." Indeed, they were "vassals." (See Volume "Concessions.")

In the Chapitoulas district above Carrollton began the great concessions of Deubreuil, Chauvin de Lèry, Chauvin de Beaulieu, Chauvin de la Frénière, St. Rayne, all large concerns worked by negro labor.

Continuing our trip up the river, on the left side, we find

in 1724 the habitations and concessions of Dartigniere & Benac, Henry Pellerin, Cousin, Vaquir, Dire (Dire leaved in Cannes Brûlées), d'Artagnan, Chautreau de Beaumont, Pujeau & Kavasse, Meran & Ferandou, Bouette, Chaval, Chesneau, Dauny, and Pierre Brou. The habitations of Chesneau and Dauny were later, after 1727, acquired by Caspas Dubs (Toups) and Ambros Heidel (Haydel), who, in 1724, were yet neighbors on the other side of the river on the German Coast.

Continuing our trip up the river, we find in 1724 the habitations of Pommier, Picollier, Sainton, Dizier, Dejean, and Pelloin. Then we meet again Germans:

Peter Schmidt, from the Palatinate. Catholic; 34 years old. His wife, his brother-in-law, aged 17 years. Three arpents cleared, which he had bought for 400 livres.

Bartholomaeus Yens (?), of Cologne. Catholic; 25 years old. A brewer. His wife, with a child at the breast. Three arpents cleared.

Then we pass the habitations of St. Pierre, St. Julien, Gobert, Reux, Caution, Guichard, Piquéry, Petit de Livilliers, Ducros, Lanthéaume. Then comes:

Joseph Ritter, of Durlach, Baden, 52 years old, a carpenter. His wife, a son of 20 years, two orphan girls of 14 and 19 years. About three years on the place. Three pigs. Works at his trade. "Is a good worker and deserves some negroes."

Then we come to the Baillifs, Claude Baillif from Picardy, and

Joseph Bailliff, of Dieux, in German Lorraine, aged 22 years. His wife. Eight arpents cleared, which he had bought for 250 livres. His widow married later Michael Zehringer, of whom we shall hear soon.

Nik. Schmitz, of Frankfurt. Catholic; 40 years of age. His wife. A daughter of 18 and one of six years. Eight arpents, which he had bought for 800 livres. "Made a good levee and is a good worker."

Peter Bayer. Catholic; 23 years old. His wife. Two arpents of land, which he had bought for 210 livres, having given up the land which he had from Governor Bienville. He brought all his things with him. Had not made more than two barrels of rice and a quantity of girammons, which was all that was left to him after paying M. Bienville. "Is a very good worker and satisfied with his small piece of land for his fortune."

Johann Fuchs, of the canton of Berne, Switzerland. Catholic; 38 years old. His wife, with a daughter at her breast. Four arpents, for which he had paid 250 livres. About one year on the place. "On account of sickness and misery he made no crop."

Lorenz Ritter, Jr., aged 20 years. Begins to establish himself on eight arpents.

From there up the left bank to where the census enumerator of 1724 stopped, there lived only Frenchmen and Canadians.

As the census of 1724, the first one to give the names of the German habitants, covers only the territory above New Orleans, and does not contain the names of the orphans staying with the German families, nor of the numerous *engagés,* many German people consequently remained unaccounted for. If the registers of the chapel on the German Coast, of which the census of 1724 speaks, and which had a resident priest as early as 1729, had not been lost, and if the records of the St. Louis Cathedral, in New Orleans, had not been to a great extent destroyed in the great fire of March 21st, 1788, many of these names could be recovered. As matters stand, only the cathedral records from 1720 to 1732 are available, which together with scattered court records and other official papers will be used here.

ADDITIONAL GERMAN NAMES OF THE PERIOD, NOT IN THE CENSUS.

There were:

MICHAEL ZEHRINGER, the progenitor of all the "Zeringue" families in Louisiana. He signed his name in German script "Michael Zehringer." He was from Franconia, Bavaria. His name appears first on the passenger list of the ship "Le Dromadaire" in 1720, together with sixty workmen under the command of de la Tour, the chief engineer of the colony. In 1721 Zehringer heads the list of "ouvriers" of the king as master carpenter. In 1722 we find Michael Zehringer in Biloxi, where in tearing down a house he found, according to a procès verbal still existing, a number of articles which had been taken away from the old fort and hidden there. In the same year his wife, Ursula Spaet, died, and, six weeks later, his daughter Salome, aged 18 years.

In the next year he married Barbara Haertel, the widow first of Magnus Albert (who came over with her in one of the pest ships) and then of Joseph Bailliff. By her Zehringer had four sons: Michael, Pierre Laurent, Joseph, and Jean Louis.

The census of 1731 mentions Michael Zehringer as living below Chapitoulas, somewhere in the Sixth District of New Orleans. His family then consisted of his wife and three children. He had one *engagé*, twelve negroes, four negresses and twenty-seven cows. He died in 1738, and one of the witnesses in his succession was Louis Wiltz.

JOHANN LUDWIG WILTZ, the progenitor of the New Orleans branch of the Wiltz family, is not mentioned in the census. Johann Ludwig Wiltz, of Eisenach, Thuringia, Germany, was born in 1711. (He wrote his name "Wilsz" as does the family in Eisenach to the present day.) In a later official document referring to the disposition of some land belonging to him, it is stated that his father-in-law, Wm. Siriac, was living on it. Siriac (see census of 1724, No. 5) had but one daughter, who, at the taking of the census of 1731 no longer lived with her parents. So the marriage of Louis Wiltz may have occurred in 1731, when Wiltz was twenty years of age. At the taking of the census of 1724, he was only thirteen years old, and he was therefore almost certainly one of the orphans whose names are not mentioned in the census of 1724.

JOHANN KATZENBERGER, who, in 1722, while yet an *engage*, married Christine "de Viceloque" (from Wiesloch, near Heidelberg, Germany), lived in the village of Gentilly, one and a half miles from New Orleans. He was from Heidelberg. In Gentilly he had an *engagé* and eight arpents of land. The name of the family has been changed into "Gasbergue."

SIMON BERLINGER, of Blaubayern in Wurtemberg, was Katzenberger's neighbor in Gentilly. He had a wife and a son, and owned eight arpents of land. His first wife was Cath. Rode, the widow of Jacob Herkomm, who had died "aux Allemands." In 1725 Berlinger married Elise Flick of Biel, Baden, whose first husband, Joseph Ziegler, had died in L'Orient. Berlinger later moved up to the German Coast.

JOHANN WEISS with his little son lived on the north shore of Lake Pontchartrain. There were then only five families with fourteen persons living on the lake shore. One of them was called "Lacombe," and it may be that "Bayou Lacombe," between Bonfuca and Mandeville, was named after that family. Descendants of this Joh. Weiss live in Pointe Coupée.

WEISSKRAEMER. Down near the mouth of the Mississippi, at a point called "Fort Balize," was the family of Weisskraemer, from Bavaria.

WICHNER. Then there were the progenitors of all the "Vicner," "Vicnair," and "Vickner" families. Nik. "Wichner" came in 1720 with his wife, Therese, and a child of one year on board the ship "L'Elephant," and was destined for the concession of Le Blanc, on the Yazoo River. His wife died some years afterward, and then he married Barbara Friedrich, the widow of Friedrich Merkel (see census of 1724, Nos. 2 and 50). The little child the Wichners brought from Germany seems to have survived, for the records of Pointe Coupée inform us that in 1777

> "Gratien Vicner (Gratian probably stands for "Christian"), the son of Nik. Vicner and Theresa . . . ' married Marie Louise Cortez", and, in the same year, a child was born to them— Marie Louise.

Sons of Nik. Wichner and Barbara Friedrich married there, too, about this time:

> 1772: Antoine Vicner, son of Nik. Vicner and Barbara Friedrich, married Perinne Cuvellier, daughter of Pierre C. and Marie Arrayo", and
> 1777: "David Vicner, son of Nik. V. and Barb. Friedrich, married Marie Margarethe Cuvellier, a sister of Perinne". She died 1781 in St. John the Baptist.

On board the same vessel by which Nik. Wichner and his family came to Louisiana there was one

FRANCOIS WICHNER, his wife Charlotte and two children,

two and four years old. Charlotte Wichner died in New Orleans in 1727, and her husband died in Pointe Coupée in 1728 as "habitant and entrepreneur."

Yet the name of this family does not appear in any census enumeration until 1731, when "Nik. Wichner, his wife and a child" are entered as habitants of Cannes Brûlées.

RICHNER (Rixner). From a petition addressed by the tutor of the children of de la Chaise to the Superior Council in 1730, we learn that one Rixner, a German, (signatures of the family prove that the original name was "Richner") had been manager of a plantation below New Orleans for three years. His time would expire in June, 1730, and a family meeting should have been called at that time to arrange for a continuance of the improvements on said plantation. In the census enumerations Johann Georg Richner appears for the first time in 1731. He lived then opposite New Orleans, two lieues above the town. There was then also a "Rixner fils," who was not yet married and who owned three negroes and three cows. Richner's daughter Margarethe married, in 1728, Jacob Kindler, a Swiss, and died the same year. Richner's wife was a sister of Ambros Heidel's mother. Johann Georg Richner came to Louisiana on board "La Saone," one of the four pest ships, in 1721. His name is not contained in the census of 1724.

SCHAF (Chauffe). Then there was the family of Schaf, of Weissenburg. Jacob Schaf and his wife Marianne sailed with five children for Louisiana on the pest ship "La Garonne" on the 24th of January, 1721. From church records it appears that the wife of Ambros Heidel (Haydel), Anna Margarethe, was a daughter of Schaf. Ambros Heidel had also a brother-in-law with him. Another daughter of Schaf married one Claireaux, and later, as her second husband, Franz Anton Steiger, from the diocese of Constance, Baden, while Anton Schaf, the eldest son, became the son-in-law of Andreas Schenck in 1737 (see census of 1724, No. 35). Yet no census mentions the Schaf family.

SCHECKSCHNEIDER. On the same ship and on the same day sailed from L'Orient the Scheckschneider family, Hans Reinhard Scheckschneider, his wife and two children. One son, Jacob, was landed in Brest and died there. Nothing more is heard of the parents, and only after 1730 their second son, Albert "Segshneider," the progenitor of the numerous Scheckschneider families appears as a habitant. He, too, must have been one of the many nameless orphans whom the census of 1724 mentions in connection with the German families.

ZWEIG (Labranche). On the 24th of January, 1721, there sailed on the pest ship "Les Deux Frères" from L'Orient a second Zweig family, Jean Zweig, with his wife and two children, who came from the neighborhood of Bamberg, Bavaria, Germany. The parents probably died before the census of 1724 was taken; their daughter was married as early as 1724 to Joseph Verret, but nothing is heard of the second child of the Zweig family, a little son,[36] until he, in 1737, bought land at what is now called "Waggaman," on the right bank of the Mississippi, opposite the habitation of his brother-in-law, Verret, who lived in "La Providence," on the left bank. There young Zweig married Susanna Marchand, of St. Marcellin, Grenoble, France, but then an orphan in the Ursuline Convent in New Orleans. The marriage contract which the author found in official acts in the custody of the "Louisiana Historical Society" was signed on the 6th of November, 1737. In this marriage contract the officiating French notary changed the name "Zweig" into "Labranche." The name Zweig being difficult to pronounce and still more difficult to write, as it contains sounds for which the French language has no signs, and young Zweig not being able to sign his name (so the contract states), it was but natural for the French notary to inquire into the meaning of the word "Zweig." Hearing that it meant in French "la branche," he put "Labranche" down as the family name of the bridegroom, and this has remained the family name ever since. The Labranche family has preserved to the present day the tradition of its German descent and of the original name "Zweig."

Having also found the joint last will and testament of Jean Zweig and Susanna Marchand made on the 21st of October, 1780, as well as the papers of the Labranche-Marchand succes-

---

[36] See *Census of 1724*: " Simon Kuhn" on Bienville's lands.

sion, settled in 1785, the writer is able to give the correct list of the children of Jean Zweig and Susanna Marchand. As to the later descendants thanks are due to Chas. Theodore Soniat Dufossat, Esq., one of the many distinguished descendants of the Labranche family, whose mother, Marie Amenaide Labranche, was a granddaughter of Michael Labranche, the eldest son of Jean Zweig.

CHILDREN OF JEAN ZWEIG (LABRANCHE) AND SUSANNA MARCHAND.

1. *Michel Labranche,* who married Louise Fortier and left seven children. He died in 1787. Female descendants married into the Le Blanc, Porthier, Sarpy, Fortier, Soniat Dufossat, Augustin, Beugnot, Wogan, Dupré, Villeré, Larendon, de la Barre, Godberry, Second, Brown, Lesseps, Oxnard, Sanchez, Chastant, and Martin families.

2. *Alexander Labranche,* one of the signers of the constitution of 1812, married a Miss Piseros and left five children. His son, Octave, became Speaker of the Louisiana House of Representatives.

   His son Alcée was also Speaker of the House of Representatives, Member of Congress, and United States Ambassador to the Republic of Texas.

   Female descendants of Alexander Labranche married into the Tricou, de la Barre, Soniat, Dufossat, Chalard, Dupuy, Meteye, Dauphine, Michel, Sarpy, Heidel (Haydel), Fortier (*a grandson of Edmund Fortier and Felicite Labranche, is Professor Alcée Fortier of the Tulane University of Louisiana*), Ganucheau, Aimé, Piseros, Villeré, Augustin, Schreiber, Toby, Frederic, Brou, Le Blanc, Grevenberg, Berault, Lalland, Blois, Wood, Jumonville, Bouligny, Albert Baldwin, and Dr. Smythe families.

3. *Jean Labranche* died single.

4. *Susanna Labranche* married Joseph Wiltz in 1759, and died in 1777. She had two children; Joseph Louis Laurent Wiltz, with whom the New Orleans branch of the Wiltz family became extinct in the male line in 1815; and Hortense Wiltz, who married, in 1789, Juan Leonardo Arnould. Their son, Julien Arnould, married (1829) Manuela Amasilie Daunoy; their daughter, Jeanne Aimee Arnould, married François Trepagnier, and their second daughter, Louise Mathilde, married Jean de Dieu Garcia.

5. *Genevieve Labranche* married Alexander Bauré.

6. *Marie Louise Labranche* married François Trepagnier.

ADDITIONAL GERMAN NAMES OF THE PERIOD NOT IN THE
CENSUS.

There were:

NIKOLAUS, CHRISTIAN and CONRAD KUGEL, three brothers,
whose parents died in L'Orient;

LOUIS LEONHARD, who married, in 1728, the daughter of
Stephan Kistenmacher;

PAUL ANTON MUELLER, of Halle, who married, in 1728,
Françoise Bourdon;

JOHANN KRETZEN, whose wife was Elise Kerner;

BERNHARD RAUCH, who died in New Orleans, in 1728, aged
fifty years;

LORENZ RAUCH;

JOHANN KECK, of Bamberg, who died in New Orleans in
1725, aged sixty years;

JOHANN WECHERS, of Strassburg, whose parents died in
Cannes Brûlées, and who was the husband of Magdalena Acker-
mann;

RUDOLPH MARTIN, whose wife was Marg. Besel, of Neu-
stadt;

JACOB STAHL;

JOHANN GEORG STAEHLE;

JOSEPH RICKER;

LORENZ GOETZ, of Dicklingen, diocese of Spite;

JOHANN STRICKER;

NIKOLAUS HUBERT;

ANDREAS TET, of Differdangen, Luxembourg, diocese of
Treve (Trier). This family still exists on Bayou Lafourche.

JOSEPH RITTER;

TINKER, of Frankfurt;

DANIEL RAFFLAND, of Berne, Switzerland;

NIKOLAUS WEISS, of Wolkringen, Berne;

JOHANNES ETTLER, of Colmar, Alsace;

JOHANN ADAM SCHMIDT;

JOHANN ADAM KINDELER, or Kindler, a Swiss;

ANTON RINGEISEN;

ADAM TRISCHL, the progenitor of all the "Triche" families;

ANTON LESCH, the progenitor of all the "Leche" and

"Laiche" families and probably a younger brother of Thomas Lesch.

DANIEL MIETSCH, of Wuerzburg;

GEORG ANTON MEMMINGER;

BALTHASAR CLAUSEN;

JACOB ECKEL, of Weilburg;

JOHANN NERLE;

GEORG RAPP;

JOHANN BAPT. MANZ, the progenitor of the "Montz" families.

All these names the author found in church records. Moreover, the census of 1724 does not contain the names of those still on Law's second plantation below English Turn. These names alone prove that the German population of Louisiana during that period was much larger than the census of 1724 would make it appear.

A CENSUS WITHOUT A DATE.

There is a census of inhabitants and their lands which is not dated. Several reasons invite the belief that this census was taken after 1732. As it gives the latest grouping, it may follow here. It will be noticed that all the Germans had left Bienville's lands, and had gone up to the German Coast on both sides of the Mississippi. In some instances the sons of the original habitants appear as landowners.

LEFT BANK.

Beginning at "La Providence" (opposite "Waggaman").

14 arpents	....	Joseph Verret, husband of M. Marg. Zweig (Labranche) ;
6 "	....	Johann Weber;
8 "	....	Louis Dubs (Toups) ;
8 "	....	Caspar Dubs (Toups) ;
15 "	....	Ambros Heidel (Haydel) ;
15 "	....	Pierre Brou;
6 "	....	Louis Champagne;
10 "	....	Jacques Antoine Le Borne.

These people being neighbors, and their children growing up together, sons of Dubs (Toups), Brou, Champagne, and Le

Borne married Heidel girls, daughters of Ambros Heidel (Haydel).

4 arpents.... Nikolaus Wichner (Vicner, Vicnaire, Vickner);
8   "   .... Daniel Hopf (Poff). Having married a second
              time, Hopf separated from his father-in-law
              Simon Kuhn, who crossed the river.

RIGHT BANK.

Beginning two miles above New Orleans, going up to the German
Villages.

10 arpents.... Johann Georg Richner (Rixner);
10   "   .... Simon Kuhn;
6   "   .... Heinrich Christman;
6   "   .... Andreas Christman;
12   "   .... Jacob Christmann;
12   "   .... Vandereck;
6   "   .... Jacon Naegeli;
4   "   .... Philipp Zahn;
6   "   .... Jacob Foltz (Folse);
5   "   .... Andreas Hofmann;
6   "   .... Christian Grabert;
5   "   .... Caspar Hegli;
8   "   .... David Meunier;
6   "   .... Jacob Rabel;
2   "   .... Jacob Weisskraemer;
8   "   .... Johann Adam Edelmeier;
9   "   .... Georg Troxler (Trosclair);
8   "   .... Georg Raeser;
6   "   .... Jacob Huber (Oubre, Ouvre, Hoover);
8   "   .... Bernhard Anton;
6   "   .... Mathias Friedrich;
6   "   .... Joseph Wagensbach (Waguespack);
6   "   .... Andreas Struempfl;
2   "   .... Peter Muench;
3   "   .... Christoph Kaiser;
3   "   .... Simon Berlinger;
1   "   .... Adam Schmidt;

3 arpents....Joseph Andrae;
6   "   ....The Presbytery;
5   "   ....Andreas Traeger (Tregre);
12   "   ....D'Arensbourg;
8   "   ....Nikolaus Meyer;
6   "   ....Jacob Ritter;
8   "   ....Adam Mattern;
6   "   ....Leonhard Magdolff;
6   "   ....Balthasar Marx;
8   "   ....Andreas Schantz (Chance);
4   "   ....Wilhelm Siriac;
4   "   ....Albert Scheckschneider;
6   "   ....Bernhard Wick;
6   "   ....Conrad Friedrich;
6   "   ....Johann Rommel;
4   "   ....Rudolph Gillen, a Swiss, and the successor of
           Johann Weber on Bienville's lands;
4   "   ....Johann Callander;
2   "   ....Johann Georg Bock;
6   "   ....Michael Vogel;
5   "   ....Martin Lambert

REINFORCEMENTS FOR THE GERMANS.

The Germans on the German Coast of Louisiana received reinforcements at different times.

In the first place the Swiss Soldiers, the majority of whom were Germans, and of whom there were always at least four companies in Louisiana during the French domination (until 1768) naturally drifted to the German Coast, and settled there at the expiration of their time of service. As stated before, the Compagnie des Indes aided them to establish themselves.

In 1754 a considerable number of people came from Lorraine, so official acts inform us, and "were settled on the German Coast." No list of names, however, is available. Governor Kerlerec wrote under date of July 4th, 1754 ("Notes and Documents," page 409):

"I have received the families from Lorraine by the 'Concord'. They are established 'aux Allemands' and work well. Many like these would be necessary for the advancement of the colony—families accustomed to working the soil, whose energies would redouble in a country where the revenues would belong to them without the burden of taxation."

In August, 1774, a large number of German families came from Frederic county, Maryland, which county had been a center of German immigration for many years. They travelled to Hagerstown, Maryland, thence through the wilderness to Fort Pitt (now Pittsburg), whence they came in boats down the Ohio and Mississippi to Manchac.

The Manchac of the Eighteenth Century was not the same locality which most of us know as the little railroad station "Manchac" on the Illinois Central Railway, 38 miles north of New Orleans. Old "Manchac" was a post on the Mississippi River, fourteen miles by river below Baton Rouge and on the same side of the Mississippi. There "Bayou Manchac," at one time called "Ascantia," and also "Iberville River," branched off from the Mississippi, and, connecting with the Amite River, Lake Maurepas and Lake Pontchartrain, formed an inland waterway from the Mississippi River to the Mississippi Sound.

It was because of this inland passage from the Mississippi to the lakes, to the gulf, and to Mobile, that Manchac was once spoken of as the proper site for the future capital of Louisiana; and when, in 1718, the present site of New Orleans was selected for that purpose, it was done principally for the reason that New Orleans, through the Bayou St. John, also has water communication with the Lake Pontchartrain and Mobile, and is much nearer to the gulf than Manchac.

Bayou Manchac was at the time of the arrival of these Germans from Maryland the boundary line between Spanish America and the English territory. It was an important waterway and trading route (especially for illicit trade with the English), and remained so until 1814, when the American General Jackson (Battle of New Orleans, January 8th, 1815) fearing that the English, by a flank movement through Lake Pontchartrain and Bayou Manchac, might enter the Mississippi and gain his rear, had the bayou filled in. "Post Manchac" was on the upper side or English bank of the bayou, while on the lower side there was a

"Spanish Fort" to defend the entrance into the Mississippi and the passage out of it. The recollection that the filling in of this bayou was a war measure still lingers with the native (Creole) population of the locality, but only dimly, for when the author asked one of those living near it when and why the bayou had been filled in, the man answered in all honesty that it was done during the "Confederate War" (1861 to 1865).

The exact locality of this historic spot where the filling in occurred can be easily found now. It is at the railroad station "Rhoades" of the Yazoo & Mississippi Valley Railway, eighty miles north of New Orleans and ten miles (railroad distance) below Baton Rouge. There is "Rhoades' Country Store" on the left or river side of the track, where, just at the station, a little ravine is seen which the railroad crosses. On the right side of the track the ravine is larger, and a little bridge leads over it. This ravine is old "Bayou Manchac." Trees have now grown up from the earth used in filling the bayou, so that the direction of the old waterway can be followed for some distance. Such historic spots as this ought to be marked by tablets to keep alive important traditions.

THE GERMANS FROM MARYLAND.

About this neighborhood the German families from Maryland settled. Judge Carrigan says in De Bow's "Review" (New Series, IV., 255 and 616): that they first took land below Hackett's Point, on the opposite side of the river, but that after several successive inundations they were compelled, in 1784, to abandon their improvements and seek refuge on the highlands (called, after them, "Dutch Highlands"):

"where their descendants yet remain, ranking among the most industrious, wealthy, and enterprising citizens of the parish."

There were many intermarriages between the Germans from Maryland and their descendants, and names of them were found by the writer in the church records of St. Gabriel, St. John the Baptist, St. James, Baton Rouge, and Plaquemine. Of these but two families will be mentioned, the two largest ones: "Kleinpeter" and "Ory."

JOHANN GEORG KLEINPETER WITH HIS WIFE GERTRUDE, FROM
MARYLAND.

"Naturales de Alemania". The entry of the marriage of his
daughter Eva, in 1777, informs us that the bride was born in Strassburg, Alsace, and so we may assume that the Kleinpeter family came
originally from that city. The family tradition says that Kleinpeter
came with six grown children to Louisiana. All were found. Gertrude Kleinpeter died in 1806, aged seventy years, and was buried in
the church yard of St. Gabriel.

CHILDREN OF JOHANN GEORG KLEINPETER AND HIS WIFE
GERTRUDE.[37]

1. *Johann Baptist Kleinpeter.* His wife was Catherine Sharp
   from Maryland.
   A. Joseph Kleinpeter married in 1822 Caroline Theresa
      Dardenne.
      a. Mathilde married in 1843 Thos. Cropper;
         Edwin Cropper married in 1869 Felicie
         Dupuy;
      b. Josephine married in 1849 Alverini Marion-
         neaux;
      c. Euphemie Henriette married in 1853 Amilcar
         Dupuy;
      d. Paul Gervais married in 1863 Pamela Isabella
         Kleinpeter, daughter of Chas. K. and Lucinde
         Cropper;
   B. Isabella Kleinpeter married in 1800 Henry Thomas,
      son of Henry Th. and Barbara Ory, all from Mary-
      land.

2. *Joseph Kleinpeter.* He married (1796) Magdalena Sharp,
   daughter of Paul Sh. and Cath. Ory, all from Maryland.
   A. Marie Rosie Kleinpeter married in 1834 Jean Michel
      Bouillon.
   B. Elisabeth Floresca Kleinpeter, baptized in 1807.

3. *Georg Kleinpeter.* He was the husband of Marg. Judith (not
   legible).
   A. Franz (François) married 1823 Adelaide Traeger
      (Tègre).
      a. A. Cornelia married in 1855 William Stokes;
      b. Francis Amelia married 1856 Thomas Byrne.
   B. Julia married 1825 Jean Traeger (Tregre), son of Jean
      T. and Eva Ory.

---

[37] The numbers, letters and distance from the margin indicate the different generations.

C. Jean married 1825 Marie Rose Bouillon.
   a. Elvira married 1851 John Huguet;
   b. Carolina married 1859 Sam. McConnell;
   c. Josiah married 1865 Elene Elder.

4. *Catharine Kleinpeter.* She came with her husband, Emmerich Adam, from Maryland.
   A. Cath. Adam, baptized 1775, married 1795 Jacob Mueller, from Maryland;
   B. Eve Adam, bapt. 1777, married 1796 Johann Thomas, son of Henry Th. and Barbara Ory, from Maryland;
      a. Georg Thomas, bapt. 1808.
   C. Marie Adam married 1805 Georg Kraus, another Marylander's son;
   D. Mathias Adam, bapt. 1782;
   E. Michael Adam, bapt. 1788.

5. *Barbara Kleinpeter.* She was the wife of Jacob Schlatter, from Maryland.
   A. Cath. Schlatter, baptized 1777;
   B. Michael Schlatter married 1814 Marie Jeanne Dardenne, and, in 1820, Marie Pamela Hawkins.
      a. Ernestine Schlatter married 1830 James Robertson;
      b. Michael Schlatter married 1843 Lodiska Desobry.

6. *Eva Kleinpeter,* the "native of Strassburg", married 1777 Johann Rein ("Reine") "of America", which here stands for Maryland. Rein signed his name in German script, as did the Kleinpeters and the Ory family.

The name Kleinpeter appears in the records sometimes in the spelling "Cloinpetre" and "Clampetre." De Bow's "Review" says (Vol. XI., 616) that Johann Georg Kleinpeter was the first to grow successfully sugar cane on the highlands. In 1790 he erected the first cotton gin, and his son, Johann Baptist Kleinpeter, in 1832, erected the first steam sugar mill.

THE ORY FAMILY.

Another large German family from Maryland was that of NIKOLAUS ORY, whose wife was ANNA STRASSBACH. She died in 1789, aged 72 years. All their children were born in Frederic county, Maryland. One of their sons, serving as a witness to a marriage in St. John the Baptist parish, signed his name in German script "Mattheis Ory, Zeig" (Zeuge=witness).

CHILDREN OF NIKOLAUS ORY AND ANNA STRASSBACH.

1. *Mathias Ory* (died 1820, aged 70 years). He married two months after the arrival of the Marylanders in Louisiana, on the 11th of October, 1774, Agnes Weber (she died 1841), daughter of Jean Weber and Weber and Cath. Traeger (Tregre), and left eleven children:
   A. Antoine Ory;
   B. Pierre Ory;
   C. Jean Louis Ory;
   D. Jean Eugene Ory;
   E. Elie Ory;
   F. Francois Ory;
   G. Jean Baptiste Ory;
   H. Joseph Ory;
   I. Marie Rose Ory, who married 1798 Georg Kamper (Cambre);
   K. Magdalena Ory, who married 1819 Pierre Himmel (Hymel);
   L. Cath. Ory, who married 1813 Jean Bapt. Baudry.

2. *Johann Ory*, married 1781 Eva Hofmann, daughter of Jacob H. and Sophie Jacob. By this his first wife he had eight children:
   A. Cath. Ory marry 1811 Francois Tircuit;
   B. Magdalena Ory married 1818 Denis Remondet;
   C. Louis Ory married 1814 Marie Picou;
   D. Marie Ory married 1814 Pierre Richard;
   E. Nik. Ory married 1821 A. Delphine Bourg;
      a. Adele Ory married 1844 Pierre Savoy;
      b. Eugenie Ory married 1844 Paul Materne;
   F. Marianne Ory, baptized 1788;
   G. Pierre Ory, baptized 1788;
   H. Jean Baptist Ory married 1808 Magdalena Weber.
         In 1797 the same Johann Ory married Barbe Tircuit, from Canada, by whom he had five children more:
   I. Juan Alexis Ory, born 1800;
   K. Felicie Ory, born 1802;
   L. Emerente Ory, born 1805, married 1827 Eugene Mattern;
   M. Francois Ory, born 1812, married 1827 M. Celestine Leche, daughter of Jean L. and Scholastica Keller;
   N. Barbara Ory, born 1797, married 1815 Jean Louis Deslattes.

3. *Louis Ory.* He married in 1791 Margarethe Wichner (Vicner), daughter of Adam W. and Anna Maria Traeger (Tregre). He died in 1800.

    A. Nikolaus Ory married in 1817 Ursula Charleville;
    B. Michael Ory, baptized in 1797;
    C. Louis Ory married 1816 Genevieve Schaf (Chauffe);
    D. Jean Baptiste Ory, baptized 1793;
    E. Marguerite Ory who married Geo. Traeger (Tregre).

4. *Barbara Ory,* the wife of Henry Thomas, from Maryland.
    A. Henry Thomas, baptized 1774, married 1800 Isabella Kleinpeter, daughter of Johann K. and Cath. Sharp.

5. *Magdalena Ory,* the wife of Philipp Jacob Engelhardt, from Maryland. This name appears in official documents in the spelling "Hingle Hart" and "Inglehart".

6. *Christine Ory,* the wife of Nikolaus Mannhofer, from Maryland.
    A. Marie Mannhofer married in 1778 Lorenz Fellmann, son of Jos. F. and Anna Wiedemann. The Fellmann family still exists on Bayou Lafourche, but the name is now changed into "Falteman", though the progenitor of the family signed his name "Lorenz Fellmann".

7. *Christian Michel Ory.* Nothing is known of him but his name. His daughter Elise married 1788 one Juan Georg.

8. *Catharine Ory,* the wife of Paul Sharp, from Maryland.
    A. Magdalena Sharp married in 1796 Joseph Kleinpeter, son of Johann Georg Kleinpeter and his wife Gertrude.
    B. Catharine Sharp married in 1781 Juan Petit Pier.

THE CREOLES OF GERMAN DESCENT.

The descendants of the founders of the German Coast and the descendants of all other Germans who came to Louisiana before the year 1803 are the "Creoles of German Descent."

Opinions as to the meaning of the word "Creole"[38] differ in Louisiana. All seem to agree that the first Louisiana Creole was born in Mobile in 1704—the child of a French father, nationality of the mother unknown. According to the census of November, 1707, the whole white population of Louisiana at that time consisted exclusively of people from France and French Canadians.

In 1719 the Germans began to arrive in Louisiana, and in-

---

[38] "The word Creole is supposed to be a negro corruption of the Spanish *criadillo,* diminutive of *criado,* a servant, follower, client; literally one bred, brought up." (*Century Dictionary.*) In the Spanish West Indies the Europeans (Spaniards) ranked first, those born in the colony second.

ternational marriages resulted. Now what was the status of the
children born in Louisiana of German parents and of those children born from international marriages?

Captain Bossu, a French officer, who, about 1750, lived in
Louisiana for several years, gives the following definition:

"We call Creoles the children born from a French father and
a French or European mother."

Bossu thus insists upon the French nationality of the father,
but the mother may be either of French or of other European
nationality, including the German. This distinction excluded the
children born in Louisiana of German parents and those children
of international marriages where the father was not a Frenchman.

But international marriages and the marriages of international children back into pure French families soon became
so numerous that the French nationality of the father, demanded
by Bossu, could no longer be insisted upon, and hence the children
of the Germans had to be admitted into full membership among
the Creoles.

Incontestible testimony for this interpretation is furnished
by the Chevalier Guy Soniat Dufossat, a French nobleman, a
marine officer, who came to Louisiana in 1751 and became the
founder of the Soniat Dufossat family in Louisiana. His testimony, being that of a man who resided permanently in Louisiana, is undoubtedly more reliable than that of Bossu, who was
but a transient observer.

Chevalier Soniat Dufossat says in his "Synopsis of the History of Louisiana," page 29:

"Creoles are defined to be the children of Europeans born in
the colony."

This includes the children born of German parents in Louisiana.

In 1765 and 1766 the Acadians came into the colony. They
were descendants of Frenchmen who had emigrated to Canada.
As Canada was a French colony, the Acadians were Creoles long
before the first Louisiana Creole was born in Mobile. Being

very ignorant and simple, however, although good people, the Acadians were not called Creoles in Louisiana, and not considered their equals by the Louisiana Creoles; for the Louisiana Creoles, at least in part, were descendants of officials of the king and of the Compagnie des Indes, and of officers, some of whom were members of noble families, whose family records date back to the time of the crusades. In their circles, as elegant education and as fine manners were to be found as in Paris.

Although the Acadians furnished Louisiana a number of excellent men, such as Governor Mouton, Chief Justice Poché, and others, and although there are family connections between them and the other Creoles, still the majority of the Acadians form a more or less separate caste, and are called to the present day "Cajuns."

In 1769 the Spaniards came. Between them and the Louisiana Creoles there was in the beginning the bitterest hatred. Later, however, came an era of reconciliation, during which the Spaniards, especially a considerable number of Spanish officers, married into Creole families. This disarmed the hatred, and the descendants of the Spaniards are now also considered Creoles.

With the year 1803, however, with the sale of Louisiana to the United States, the admission of new elements of the population into the Creole class ceased. Louisiana was now no longer a colony, and the large immigration setting in at that time from the United States into Louisiana did not come from Europe. The descendants of the Americans are therefore not called Creoles.

Yet the Americans continued to use the word "Creole" for commercial purposes, and to apply it to everything coming from Louisiana, negroes, animals, and goods of all kinds. "Creole negroes" are negroes born in Louisiana; and we hear likewise of "Creole chickens," "Creole eggs," "Creole ponies," "Creole cows," "Creole butter," and so forth. As a trade mark "Creole" signifies the home-raised or home-made, the better and fresher goods in contrast to those imported from the West, from the North, or from Europe.

After what has been said, we may now proceed to define the word "Creole:"

Creoles are the descendants of the white people who emi-grated from Europe to Louisiana during the colonial period, i. e., before 1803; and are properly only those born within the limits of the original territory of Louisiana.
Great stress is to be laid on the word "white," as there are many persons, especially in other parts of the United States, who, from lack of better information, suspect the Louisiana Creoles of having in their veins a tincture of African or of Indian blood, possibly both, along with the Caucasion. Such a suspicion may be justified as regards the Spanish Creoles of the West Indies, Central America, Mexico, and South America, for the Spanish colonists there did not always preserve the purity of their race.

But Louisiana was a *French* colony, where, as early as 1724, the celebrated "Black Code" was promulgated, which regu-lated the relations between the whites and the blacks, forbade marriages between them, and imposed heavy fines for violations. Even sexual intercourse outside of marriage was forbidden; and when a negress, a slave, had a child by her white master, the master had to pay a fine of 300 livres, and the negress with her child became the property of the hospital of New Orleans. In addition to the legal punishment, such connections were always followed by social ostracism and the refusal of the family to recognize the issue of such marriages and illicit relations; and to the present day every Creole family will absolutely refuse to receive any person on terms of equality whose family at any time, no matter how remote, was tainted by the blood of the black race. It is true that there are many colored people in Louisiana who bear names of Creole families, but this can, in many instances, be explained by the fact that slaves voluntarily freed by their owners, often adopted the family names of their former masters.

The definition of the word "Creole" given above is further supported by what Gayarré says:

"Creoles we call the children of European parents in Spanish or French colonies."

That some of the Creoles of the present generation are not satisfied with the author's definition was shown in 1886, when an attempt was made to found a "Creole Association" in New Orleans, upon which occasion it became necessary to define the word "Creole."

Henry Rightor in his "Standard History of New Orleans," page 195, says that he found in the papers of this association, which has since been dissolved, two definitions which undoubtedly represent the views of the founders of the "Creole Association." The first one is:

"The Louisiana Creole is one who is a descendant of the original settlers in Louisiana under the French and Spanish governments, or, generally, one born in Louisiana of European parents, and whose mother-tongue is French."

As this definition, however, would have excluded the descendants of the Spanish colonists, who preserved their mother-tongue, a second attempt at a definition seems to have been made:

"A native descendant of European parents speaking French or Spanish."

It is, therefore, intended now to make the preservation of the mother-tongue the test, and the vice-president of the "Creole Association" made this clear when he, in the absence of the president, Chief Justice Poché, said in his inauguration speech:

"Let no man, repudiating the tongue in which his first prayers were lisped, join us."

If this view, to determine one's descent by the adherence to the mother-tongue, were correct, nothing could be said against calling now, as some partisans really do, all Creoles "French Creoles," for all Creoles speak French now. But then the question would necessarily occur:

What, then, if the descendants of the present Creoles in fifty, or one hundred years from now should no longer speak French, but English? Will there then be no more Creoles?

It stands to reason that one's mother-tongue cannot decide the question of one's descent. The mother-tongue never decides in matters of descent. In a succession case no judge would ever think of basing his decision upon the mother-tongue of the claimants, and of the many millions of people who immigrated from Europe to the United States no descendant ever forfeited his right of inheritance on account of his having adopted English in place of the mother-tongue of his family.

In matters of descent not the language but the *blood* is the vital matter, and the blood alone. We must therefore classify the Louisiana Creoles according to the blood of their progenitors, and say:

There are

Creoles of French descent,

Creoles of German descent,

Creoles of Spanish descent,

and still others, for instance Creoles of Irish descent (the Mc-Carty family) and Creoles of Scotch descent (the Pollock family).

WHAT IS THE PROBABLE NUMBER OF THE CREOLES OF GERMAN DESCENT?

This question may be answered in the words of the promise, given to Abraham: they are as numerous "as the sands on the sea shore."

The church registers of St. John the Baptist prove that the German pioneers were blessed with enormously large families. It seems that heaven wanted to compensate them in this manner for the many dear ones they had lost in the ports of France, on the high seas, in Biloxi, and during the first period of their settling in Louisiana. I found fourteen of them, sixteen, eighteen, and once even twenty-two children in a family.

Yet, in spite of this great number of children there was no difficulty in providing for the numerous daughters. There was a great scarcity of women in Louisiana in early times. Indeed, as we have seen, prostitutes were gathered in Paris and sent to Louisiana to provide wives for the colonists. Few of these lewd women ever had any children, and their families became extinct in the second and third generation. See census of 1721 where it is stated that fourteen soldiers were married but that there was not a single child in these fourteen families.

According to this census—when the Germans on the German Coast and those on the Arkansas River were not enumerated—there were only thirty women with 21 children for every hundred white men in the district of New Orleans. No wonder that the young Frenchmen, especially those of the better class, chose wives from among the German maidens, who were not only morally and physically sound and strong, but had also been reared by their German mothers to be good house-wives.

Of the Heidel (Haydel) family, whose descendants are so numerous that one of them told the writer: "My family alone can populate a whole parish (county) in Louisiana," female descendants of the first five generations married into seventy-four different French families, and it very seldom happened that there was but one marriage between two families. Remember that in these statistics are still wanting the entries of the many registers that were burned at the "Red Church" and those of the volumes burned with the cathedral of New Orleans in 1788.

Yes, even into the most exclusive circles, into the families of the officials and of the richest merchants the German girls married, they became the wives of French and Spanish officers of ancient nobility in whose descendants German blood still flows.

Only one example: female descendants of Karl Friedrich D'Arensbourg married into the families of de la Chaise, de la Tour, de la Grue, de Villeré, de L'Home, de Vaugine, d'Olhond, Laland d'Apremont, de Bosclair, de Livaudais, de Blanc, de la Barre, de Léry, de la Vergne, de Buys, Forstall, Trudeau, Perret, St. Martin, Montegut, Lanaux, Beauregard, Bouligny, Suzeneau, le Breton, Tricou, Duverjé, Urquhart, de Reggio, Rathbone, Durel, Luminais, Bermudez.

When General O'Reilly, in the year 1769, forced the Spanish yoke upon Louisiana, he selected six of the most prominent citizens, whom he had shot in order to intimidate the hostile population. Of these six "martyrs of Louisiana," were not fewer than three who had wives from German families:

JOSEPH MILHET, the richest merchant of the colony, had as his wife Margarethe Wiltz, whose father was from Eisenach, in Thuringia, while her mother was born in Frankenthal, Saxony;

MARQUIS, the commander-in-chief of the insurgents, was married to a daughter of an Alsatian officer, Gregor Volant, from Landsee, near Strassburg, and

JOSEPH DE VILLERÉ, under whose command the Germans of the German Coast had marched against the Spanish in 1768, had a grandchild of Karl Friedrich D'Arensbourg as his wife.

THE GERMAN LANGUAGE AMONG THE CREOLES OF LOUISIANA.

As a rule, the German girls took German husbands, and whole families married into one another. To give but one example, it may be mentioned here that out of the ten children of one Jacob Troxler not fewer than eight married into the Heidel (Haydel) family. In such families the German language survived longest, and old Creoles of German descent have told me that their grandparents still understood and were able to speak the German language, although they were not able to read and write it, as there were never any German teachers on the German coast. I myself found among the old records a building contract of 1763 written in German, in which one Andreas Bluemler, a carpenter, obligated himself to build "for 2000 livres and a cow, a heifer and a black calf," a house for Simon Traeger (Tregre). A law-suit followed and so this building contract, together with the court records of the case were preserved to the present day.

In consequence, however, of the many family ties between the Germans and the French, and in consequence of the custom of the Creoles to marry into related families, French gradually became the family language even in those German families which had preserved the German language during three generations.

Some few German words, however, can occasionally be heard even yet in the Creole families of German descent, especially words relating to favorite dishes, "which our grandmother was still able to cook, but which are no longer known in our families."

German names of persons, too, have been preserved, although in such a mutilated form that they can hardly be recognized. Thus the tradition in the Heidel (Haydel) family is that the first Heidel born in Louisiana was called "Anscopp," with the French nasal pronunciation of the first syllable. I could not get the original German for "Anscopp" until I compiled the genealogy of the family when I found that the first Heidel born in Louisiana was christened "Jean Jacques." Now I knew that they called him in the family "Hans Jacob," and that by throwing out the initial "h" and contracting "Hans Jacob" the name was changed into "Anscopp." In a similar manner "Hans Peter" was changed into "Ampete" and "Hans Adam" in to "Ansdam."

The German language disappeared quickest in families where a German had married a French girl. There no German was spoken at all, and even the Christian names customary in German families disappeared even as early as in the second generation, as now also the French wife and her relatives had to be considered in the giving of names to the children. Instead of Hans Peter, Hans Jacob, Michl, Andre, and Matthis, the boys of the German farmers were now called: Sylvain, Honoré, Achille, Anatole, Valcourt, Lezin, Ursin, Marcel, Symphorion, Homer, Ovide, Onésiphore, and Onesime; and instead of the good old German names Anna Marie, Marianne, Barbara, Katharine, Veronika, and Ursula, the German girls were called: Hortense, Corinne, Elodie, Euphémie, Félicité, Melicerte, Désiré, Pélagie, Constance, Pamela; and after the French revolution each family had her "Marie Antoinette."

The Fate of the German Family Names Among the Creoles.

The changes which the German family names underwent among the Creoles are most regrettable. Without exception, all names of the first German colonists of Louisiana were changed, and most of the Creoles of German descent at the present time no longer know how the names of their German ancestors looked. Sometimes they were changed beyond recognition, and only by tracing some thirty families with all their branches through all the church records still available; by going through eighty boxes of official documents in the keeping of the "Louisiana Historical Society;" by ransacking the archives of the city of New Orleans

and of a number of country parishes, and by compiling the genealogies of these families has the author been able to recognize the
German people of the different generations, to ascertain their
original names, and to connect the old German settlers with the
generation of the Creoles of German descent now living.

Various circumstances contributed to the changing of these
names. The principal one was, no doubt, the fact that some of
the old German colonists were not able to write their names.
Their youth had fallen into the period of the first fifty years
after the "Thirty Years' War" and into the last years of the
war when the armies of Louis XIV of France devastated the
Palatinate. In consequence of the general destruction and the
widespread misery of that period, schools could hardly exist in
their homes. It was therefore not the fault of these people if
they could not read and write their names. Moreover, as the
parents could not tell their children in Louisiana how to write
their names, these children had to accept what French and Spanish teachers and priests told them, and what they found in official
documents. But French and Spanish officials and priests heard
the German names through French and Spanish ears, and wrote
them down as they thought these sounds should be written in
French or Spanish. Moreover, Spanish and French officials and
priests at that early time were not great experts in the grammar
of their own language.

Finally, the early German colonists did not pronounce their
own names correctly, but according to their home dialect.

To prove the last assertion three German names shall be
considered: *"Schaf," "Schoen," "Manz."* In South Germany,
where most of these people came from, "a" is pronounced broad,
and almost approaches the "o." The South German peasant
does not say "meine Schafe," but "mei' Schof." No wonder that
the French officials spelled the name "Schaf" "Chauffe." In this
form the name still exists in Louisiana.

"Schoen" was evidently pronounced like German "Schehn,"
for which reason the French spelled it "Chesne," "Chaigne," and
"Chin."

And the name "Manz" for the same reason was changed into
"Montz."

Many changes in the spelling of the German names follow the general "Law of the mutation of Consonants," called Grimm's Law, which may be roughly stated thus: "Consonants uttered by the same organ of speech are frequently interchanged."

Lip sounds: b, p, v, f, ph, (English) gh (as in the word "enough");

Tongue sounds: d, t, s, z, sch, (French) ch, che, c, and x;

Throat sounds: g, k, ch, hard c, qu, (French) gu, (Spanish) j and x.

Original German
form of name:

Weber..............	changed into Veber, Vebre, Vever, Bevre, Febre, Webere, Febore, Vabure, Weibre, Weyber, Febore and now "Webre".
Kremser	Chremser.
Kamper.............	Kammer, Campert, Camper, Campfer, Cambra (Spanish) and now "Cambre".
Krebs	Creps.
Kindler.............	Kindeler, Quindler, Quinler.
Kerner.............	Cairne, Kerne, Querne, Kerna, Carnel, Quernel.
Kindermann.........	Quinderman, Quindreman.
Clemens............	Clement.
Buerckel............	Pircle, Percle, Bercle, Birquelle, Pircli, Lerkle and Percler.

One Marianne Buerckel married one "Don Santiago Villenol". As the bridegroom's own signature proves, the man's name was not "Santiago Villenol" but "Jacob Wilhelm Nolte".

Buchwalter..........	Bucvalter, Bouchevaldre, Boucvaltre.
Willig..............	Willique, Villique, Vilic, Villig, Billic, Velyk.
Katzenberger........	Katcebergue, Kastzeberg, Cazverg, Casverg, Casberg, Cazimbert, Kalsberke, Casvergue, Castleberg, Katsberk, Cazenbergue and now "Casbergue".
Wichner............	Wichnaire, Vicner, Vicnaire, Vickner, Vignel, Vichneair, Vighner, Vequenel, Vicgner, Vigner, Vuquiner, Bicner, Vixner, Wicner, Wickner.

In an entry in the marriage register of 1791, which four members of this family signed, the name Wichner is spelled differently five times, as the officiating priest, too, had his own way of spelling it.

Wagensbach.........Vagensbach, Wagenspack, Wagenpack, Vaglespaque, Vaverspaqhez, Waiwaipack, Wabespack, Bangepach, Varesbach, Vacbach, Wabespack, Woiguespack, Woiwioguespack, Vacheba, Vacquensbac, Weghisbogh and now "Waguespack".

Trischl.............Tris, Trisch and now "Triche".

Traeger............Draeger, Tregle, Graeber, Trecle, Traigle, Treigle, Treguer, Draigue, Dreiker, Draeguer, and now "Tregre".

Ettler..............Etlair, Edeler, Edler, Ideler, Heidler, Idelet, Edtl. Johannes Ettler used to add to his signature "from Colmar". From this came "dit Colmar", "alias Colmar", and when his daughter Agnes Ettler died, she was entered into the death register of St. John the Baptist "Ines Colmar".

Foltz...............Foltse, Faulse, Folst, Folet, Folch, Folsh, Poltz, Fols and now "Folse".

Manz...............Mans,. Mons, Monces, Months, Munts and now "Montz".

Wilsz..............Wils, Vils, Willst, Vills, Vylzt, Vylts, Wuells, Bilce, Veilts. The Wilsz family in Eisenach, Thuringia, Germany, writes the name with "sz", and so did Ludwig Wilsz, the progenitor of the New Orleans branch of the family, but his brother in Mobile adopted "tz" as did all descendants of both branches, including Governor Wiltz of Louisiana.

Lesch..............Leche, Laiche, Lesc, Leichet, Lecheux and now "Leche" and "Laiche".

Zehringer...........Seringuer, Sering, Seringue, Zerinck, Zerincque, Ceringue and now "Zeringue".

Huber..............Houbre, Houber, Houver, Ubre, Ouuere, Ouvre, Houvre, Hoover, Vbre and Vbaire. In "Vbre" and "Vbaire" the "V" stands for "U".

Initial "h" is prounounced neither in French nor in Spanish. For this reason initial "h" in German names was usually dropped, and where an attempt was made to represent it, the French often used "k," while the Spaniards represented it by "x" or "j," and occasionally by "qu."

Heidel changed into..Aydel, Jaidel, Keidel. Appears also as Hedelle, Idel, Etdell and is now "Haydel".

Richner............Rixner, Risner, Resquiner, Ristener.

Himmel.............Immel, Ymelle, Ximel, Quimel and now "Hymel".
Wichner.............Vixner.
Helfer..............Elfer, Elfre, Elfert.
Hufnagel...........Oufnague, Houfnack.
Hauser.............Hoser, Oser.

When a German name began with a vowel they often prefixed an "h":

Engel...............Engle, Aingle, Ingle, Yngle, Hingel, Hincle, Hengel, Heigne and now "Hingle".
Engelhardt.........Hingle Hart, Hanglehart, Inglehart.
Edelmeier..........Heldemaire, Aidelmer, Eldemere, Delmaire, Le Maire.

In Spanish the letter "l" occurs sometimes when we expect an "r," for instance "Catalina" for "Catherina." So the Spanish use "l" also in family names instead of "r":

> Quernel instead of Kerner,
> Beltram for Bertram,
> Viquinel and Vignel for Vicner (Wichner),
> Tregle for Traeger (Tregre).

By replacing German "sch" by "ch," as was the custom during the French period, the German names assumed an entirely foreign appearance, as no German word ever begins with "ch":

Schantz.............Chance and Chans;
Strantz.............Schrantz, Chrence;
Schwab.............Chave and Chuabe, Chuave;
Schaf..............Chauff, Cuave, Cheauf, Chof, Chofe, Choff, Chaaf, Soff, Shoff, Skoff, Shaw, Chaaf and now "Chauffe";
Schaefer...........Chefer, Cheffre, Chevre, Chepher, Cheper, Scheve.
Schmidt............Chemitt and Chmid;
Schuetz............Chutz.

The German "o" became "au" and "eau":

Vogel..............Fogle, Feaugle, Voguel, and Fauquel.
Hofmann ....Ofman, Aufman, and Eaufman.

Also the inclination of the French to put the stress upon the last syllable appears in German names:

Himmel.............Ymelle;
Heidel.............Aydelle, Hedelle, Haydelle, Etdelle.
Rommel............Rommelle. Appears also in the forms Rommle, Romle, Rome, Romo (Spanish), Romme, Rom.

OTHER INTERESTING CHANGES.

Troxler changed into..Stroxler, Stroscler, Drozeler, Troesscler, Troxlaire, Drotseler, Trocsler, Trucksler, Trouchsler, Troustre, Troseler, Trocler, Trossclaire, Troscler, Trocher, Drotzeler, Droezler, Troxclair, Troslisser.

Kuhn...............Coun, Cohn, Koun.

Mayer..............Mayre, Maller, Mahir, Mahier, Maieux, Meyier, Mayeux.

Dubs...............Tus, Touptz, Toubse, Toupse, Tups, now "Toups".

Ory................Orji, Oray, Orij, Haury, Aury.

Keller..............Queller, Caler, Keler, Quellar. One "Don Juan Pedro Cuellar" signed his name in German script "Hansbeter Keller".

Held................Haid, Helder, Helette, Hail, Helle, Helte.

Steilleder...........Stelider, Steilledre, Stillaitre, Stillaite, Stilet, Estilet, Steili, Steli now "Estilet".

Steiger.............Stayer, Stahier, Sther, Stayre, Steili, Stayer, Steygre, Estaidre.

Jansen..............Yentzen, Hentzen, Kensin.

Kleinpeter...........Cloinpetre, Clampetre.

Ketterer............Quaitret.

Hans Erich Roder...Anseriquer Auder.

Weisskraemer........Visecrenne.

Struempfl...........Strimber, Estrenfoul.

Hansjoerg...........Hensiery.

Graef(in)..........Crevine.

Kissinger...........Guzinguer, Quisingre.

Urban Ohnesorg......Hour Pamonscaurse.

Dorothea Baer (in)...Torotay Perrinne.

Miltenberger.........Mil de Bergue.

Christmann..........Crestman, Yresman, Krestman.

Wenger.............Vinguer.

Bendernagel.........Bintnagle.

Wehrle.............Verlet, Verlay.

Schoderbecker.......Chelaudtre, Chloterberk.

Renner.............Rinher.

Also Christian names as well as the names of places (see Ettler, from Colmar) and nicknames became family names.

The daughter of one Jacob Helfer was entered into the marriage register as "Mademoiselle Yocle," because her father was called familiarly "Jockel," which is a nickname for Jacob.

The family of Thomas Lesch was for some time lost to me until I recovered it under the name of "Daumas"="Thomas."

Remarkable was the fate of the name "Hofmann." The forms Ofman, Aufman, Eaufman, Haufman, Ophman, Oghman, Ocman, Hochman, Haukman, Hacmin, Aupemane, Augman, Olphman, and Ocmane were not the only changes that occurred. The family came from Baden and thus "de Bade" was often added to the name. In course of time the people forgot the meaning of "de Bade," and a new name was formed, "Badeau," with a feminine form, "Badeauine."

The eldest daughter of one Hofmann married a man by the name of "Achtziger." This name seems to have given a great deal of trouble. I found "Hacksiger," "Chactziger," "Oxtiger," "Oxtixer," "Axtigre," "Harzstingre," "Astringer," "Haxsitper," and "Horticair," but early the French officials (like in the case "Zweig-Labranche") translated the name Achtziger into French "Quatrevingt," to which they were in the habit of adding the original name as best they knew how. Now, as the eldest daughter of this Hofmann was called "Madame Quatrevingt," they seem to have called her younger sister in a joking way "Mademoiselle Quarante," for when she married she appears in the church register as "Mademoiselle Quarantine," alias "Hocman."

Finally, another name shall be mentioned here, which is now pronounced "Sheckshnyder." The legend is that six brothers by the name of "Schneider" came across the sea, and each one of them was called "one of the six Schneiders," hence the name "Sheckshnyder;" but this legend is, like many another legend, false. The first priest of St. John the Baptist, the German Capuchin father Bernhard von Limbach (1772), who wrote even the most difficult German names phonetically correct, entered the name as "Scheckschneider," which is an old German name. The progenitor of this family, Hans Reinhard Scheckschneider, is mentioned on the passenger list of one of the four pest ships which sailed from L'Orient on the twenty-fourth of January, 1721. There were no "six Schneider" on board, only he, his wife and two sons, one of whom died in Brest. Yet he was already called "Chezneider," even on board ship. From this came later the following forms, which were all taken from official documents:

Sexchneyder, Sexnaidre, Snydre, Sixtailleur, Seckshneyder, Secxnauder, Sheknaidre, Seinadre, Seicnaydre, Schnaidre, Seicshnaydre, Seishaudre, Schgnaidre, Seinaydre, Scheixneydre, Sixney, Sexnall, Chesnaitre, Caxnayges, Cheixnaydre, Chexnaydre, Ceixnaidre, Chixnaytre, Segsneidre, Cheesnyder, Celfceneidre, Hexnaider.   At present almost every branch of this very numerous family writes the name differently.

German Names in the Spanish Marriage Register of St. John the Baptist.

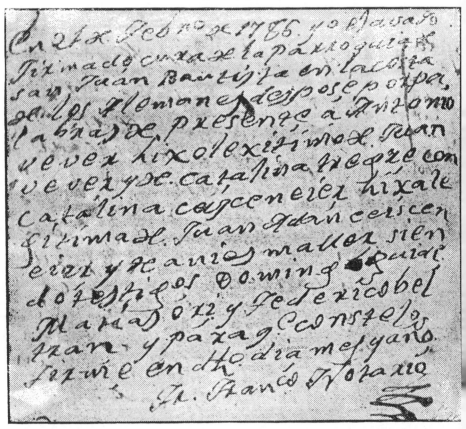

Free translation: On the 21st of February 1785 Anton Weber, legitimate son of John Weber and Cath. Traeger (Tregre), married Cath. Scheckschneider, legitimate daughter of John Adam Scheckschneider and Agnes Mayer. Witnesses: Domingo Guide, Mathias Ory and Fred. Bertram.

Frater Francesco, Notario.

CONCLUSION.

The Creoles of German descent constitute even now a large, if not the largest, part of the white population of the German Coast, the parishes of St. Charles and St. John the Baptist, of Louisiana. But they spread at an early time, also, over neighboring districts, where their many children took up new lands for cultivation.

They went up to St. James parish, where some connected themselves with the Acadian families by marriages. They also went to the parishes of Assumption, Ascension, and Iberville, still further up the Mississippi. They went to where Donaldsonville now stands. On that place was the village of the Chetimachas Indians; and Bayou Lafourche, which there branches off from the Mississippi and extends for a distance of 110 miles to the Gulf of Mexico, was then called "Fourche des Chetimachas."

Down this bayou the descendants of the early Germans pressed and throughout the whole length of Bayou Lafourche I found many German names in the church registers of Donaldsonville, Paincourtville, Plattenville, Napoleonville, Labadieville, Thibodeaux, Houma and Lockport. Also the word "Teche" (Bayou Teche) is supposed to be derived from "Deutsch."

In the course of time, however, great changes have occurred among the descendants of the early Germans, though not so much in their physical appearance. There are still among them many of the ancient stalwart German type, who betray the French blood received in the course of time only by their more lively disposition; their are still blue eyes and blond hair among them, although in some families both types, the German and the Latin, seem to be equally represented; there is still the same very large number of children to be found in their families; the Creole of German descent is still the most robust of the Creoles, and one very well known family still produces the same giants as in the days when their German great-grandfathers used to drive off the Acadians, when they came down from St. James to disturb the Saturday dances on the German Coast.

The changes spoken of refer chiefly to their economical condition. Through the Civil War many of these families lost not only their slaves, but also their plantations, the source of their once very considerable wealth. They have, therefore, shared the lot of the other Creoles. But, thanks to their inherited energy, they wrung an existence from the adverse conditions, and now that a new era of prosperity has dawned upon Louisiana, their prospects, too, have become brighter—many of them are now to be found in the professions, in commercial and industrial pursuits, and in official positions all over the State, in which they have invariably gained for themselves an enviable reputation, and often great distinction; others made use of their knowledge of planting by accepting after the war positions of managers of large estates, later renting and finally buying some of the many vacant plantations, and still others succeeded in preserving and increasing the ante bellum wealth of their families. The great majority of the Creoles of German descent may be said to be again on the road to prosperity.

But their golden age is passed, and will never return in the form in which they once enjoyed it. This they know, and for this reason their mind, especially that of the older generation, reverts with tender regret to the past. They also still remember their German descent, and when they now look sadly upon the land which their ancestors had conquered from the wilderness and the Mississippi, and which also once belonged to them, but which is now tilled by others, they still say with pride:

"WE ARE THE DESCENDANTS OF THOSE GERMANS WHO TURNED THE WILDERNESS INTO A PARADISE SUCH AS LOUISIANA NEVER POSSESSED BEFORE."

May they ever remember their German ancestors and emulate their example!

Official Acknowledgment
OF THE
Worth and Value of the German Pioneers of Louisiana.

Laussat, colonial prefect of Louisiana and commissioner of the French government in 1803, wrote the following letter:

New Orleans, Messidor 6th. Eleventh Year.[88a]
The Colonial Prefect of Louisiana
 to Citizen Chaptal,
  Minister of the Interior.

Citizen Minister:

I received the letter of the 4th of Floreal of this year by which your Excellency deigned to consult me on the project of embarking German laborers for Louisiana.

This is a project which should be made a regular system by the French government for several years if it wants to derive profit from this country and to preserve it.

Its present condition and its wretched (*misérable*) population demand this imperatively. This class of peasants, and especially of that nationality, is just the class we need and the only one which always achieved perfect success in these parts.

What is called here the "German Coast" is the most industrious (*la plus industrieuse*), the most populous (*la plus peuplée*), the most at ease (*la plus aisée*), the most upright (*la plus honnête*), the most respected (*la plus éstimée*) part of the inhabitants of this colony.

I regard it as essential that the French government should make it a rule to send every year from one thousand to twelve hundred families of the frontier departments of Switzerland, the Rhine and Holland; the emigrants of our southern provinces are not worth anything (*n'y valent rien*).

Laussat.

(*Évènements de* 1803, page 315. New Transcripts of the Louisiana Historical Society.)

[88a] The month of Messidor was the harvest month. It began on the 19th of June and ended on the 18th of July. The eleventh year was the year 1803.

APPENDIX.

The German Waldeck Regiment
and
The Sixtieth or "Royal American Regiment on Foot"
in the War of 1779 to 1781.

Although not bearing on the history of the settlement of the German Coast of Louisiana, a short account is added here of the part which the German Waldeck regiment and the 60th or Royal American regiment took in the Anglo-Spanish War of 1779-1781. This war belongs to the colonial history of Louisiana; and as this work deals with the Germans of that period, the German soldier who fought on Louisiana soil in colonial times and there, no doubt, also met the German pioneer, may justly claim some space in this book.

During the War of Independence England secured from some of the smaller principalities of Germany auxiliary troops which fought on the English side. There was no political alliance between these principalities and England, it was traffic in human flesh, pure and simple. England rented these troops to fight for her, paid a good rental for them, and a fixed price for every soldier killed or wounded. To the honor of the great majority of the German monarchs be it said that they strongly disapproved of this traffic, and that the King of Prussia openly favored the American cause and forbade the English auxiliary troops to march through his kingdom.

There were 29,166 German soldiers in the English army:

Hesse-Cassel	furnished	16,992	men	of	whom	she	lost	6,500;
Brunswick	"	5,723	"	"	"	"	"	3,015;
Hanau	"	2,422	"	"	"	"	"	981;
Ansbach Bayreuth	"	1,644	"	"	"	"	"	461;
Waldeck	"	1,225	"	"	"	"	"	720;
Anhalt-Zerbst	"	1,160	"	"	"	"	"	176;

29,166

11,853

The very great loss in men was due in part to the fact that a great number of these German soldiers, on coming into contact with the Germans living in America, who were loyal Americans, and of whom many thousands fought in the revolutionary army under Washington, were persuaded to abandon the English cause and settled in this country.

In May, 1779, hostilities broke out between Spain and England; and the boundary line between the English and the Spanish possessions in America—the Mississippi River, Bayou Manchac, the Amite River, and Lakes Maurepas and Pontchartrain—became a scene of war, and some of the principal actors were German troops.

The English held Fort Panmure, where Natchez now stands; a post on Thompson's Creek, near the present Port Hudson; Fort New Richmond, now Baton Rouge; Fort Bute, on the Mississippi, at the entrance into Bayou Manchac; a post on the Amite River, presumably "French Settlement," below the confluence of Bayou Manchac and Amite River and Big Colyell Creek and Amite River; Mobile, and Pensacola. In order to strengthen these positions the English sent some of their auxiliary troops, the German Waldeck regiment, from New York by way of Jamaica to Pensacola, where they landed on the twenty-ninth of January, 1779.

Here the Waldeckers met a company of German recruits belonging to the 16th regiment, eight companies of the "Royal American Regiment on Foot," also known as the 60th English regiment, and some royalists from Maryland and Pennsylvania.

The 60th regiment was raised by order of the Parliament in 1755. "The men were chiefly Germans and Swiss who had settled in America. They were all zealous Protestants and, in general, strong, hardy men, accustomed to the American climate and, from their religion, language and race particularly proper to oppose the French."[39] As they could not speak English, however, it became necessary to grant commissions to a number of foreign Protestants who had served abroad as officers or engineers and

---

[*] J. G. Rosengarten: *The German Soldier in the Wars of the United States;* Philadelphia, 1890, pages 15 to 24.

spoke the German language. On the fifteenth of June, 1756, forty German officers came to America to serve in this regiment. The Rev. Michael Schlatter, the head of the Reformed German Church in America, was the chaplain of this regiment from 1756 to 1782. While in Pensacola, the 60th regiment still consisted "mainly of Germans."

The English forces on the Mississippi being only 500 men, under Lieutenant Colonel Dickson, who urgently called for reinforcements, part of the 60th regiment and the grenadier company of the Waldeckers left Pensacola for the Mississippi on the nineteenth of June, 1779. On the second of August Major von Horn, with his company of Waldeckers and fifteen men of the company of Colonel Hanxleden, followed, and on the thirtieth of the same month another company of Waldeckers, that of Captain Alberti. They went by way of Lake Pontchartrain, Amite River and Bayou Manchac.

The Spanish in New Orleans succeeded in capturing some of the English transports on Lake Pontchartrain, among which was the vessel which carried the company of Captain Alberti, who, with his officers, three sergeants, one drummer and forty-nine privates, was taken prisoner and brought to New Orleans, where he died of fever on the twenty-first of July, one day after Lieutenant von Goren had died of the same disease.

On the twenty-second of August, 1779, the Spanish Governor Galvez left New Orleans with a force of 1430 men and a small gun fleet to attack the English posts on the Mississippi. On his approach, the main force of the English withdrew towards Baton Rouge, leaving in Fort Bute Captain von Haake with a detachment of twenty Waldeckers. A recent history of Louisiana says that Galvez took this post by "assault," and even gives the name of the first Creole to enter the fort. There cannot have been much fighting at Fort Bute. From the fact that only eight prisoners were taken by Galvez, and the further fact that Captain von Haake later fought in Baton Rouge, it seems probable that this officer, on hearing of the large force marching against him, withdrew from Fort Bute, leaving a few men behind to make a show of resistance and hereby detain Galvez for a few days on his march to Baton Rouge. In this they seem to have succeeded, as Galvez waited five days before ordering the "assault."

Then he pressed on to Baton Rouge, which he also intended to take by assault; but after losing 500 men in the first, and 140 in a subsequent assault in which he was even compelled to withdraw his batteries, he concluded to invest the post. Lieutenant Colonel Dickson was not prepared to resist a regular siege, and as many of his men were sick, an honorable surrender was arranged. The English left Baton Rouge with all the honors of war, drums beating and banners flying. The prisoners were to be taken first to New Orleans and thence transported to New York, and were not to fight again within eighteen months. Every officer retained his sword and every man his private property.

Of the Waldeckers two captains, three lieutenants, three surgeons, eight sergeants, six drummers, three servants, and 176 privates surrendered in Baton Rouge. Ensign Nolting and one private fell. Lieutenant Leonhardi, who had distinguished himself during the two assaults of the Spaniards, died of his wounds on the Mississippi while being conveyed to New Orleans. One surgeon, two non-commissioned officers and nineteen privates died of their wounds; and one officer and six privates were slightly wounded. Of the other troops fighting on the side of the English, 216 surrendered.

From letters written by German officers, then prisoners of war in New Orleans, and from published diaries, we learn that many of the Waldeckers died in this city, and that many were "still sick." Lieutenant Strubberg, in a letter to a brother officer in Pensacola, speaks very highly of Governor Galvez, who often invited the German officers to dinner, and even allowed them to visit their comrades in Pensacola. "The people of New Orleans, too," he says, "were very friendly and kind."

Meanwhile, Governor Galvez went with a large fleet and a landing army to Mobile, which was ill prepared to resist an attack, and which surrendered after a breach had been made in the walls of the fort, on the fourteenth of March, 1780, before the men of the 60th regiment and the rest of the Waldeckers sent from Pensacola for the relief of that town could reach there. The relief column consisted of 522 men. It returned to Pensacola on the nineteenth of March.

This expedition from Pensacola to Mobile—72 miles in incessant rain and over soft soil, "not a human dwelling, and at night surrounded by wild beasts"—is described by the Waldeckers as one of their greatest hardships. They also complained of the poor fare in Pensacola.

Chaplain Steuernagel writes: "In the morning we drink a glass of water and eat a piece of bread; at noon we have nothing to drink but water, and our supper consists of a pipe of tobacco and a glass of water." A ham was sold for seven dollars, a pound of tobacco cost four dollars, a pound of coffee one dollar and a "Mass" (about one liter) of whiskey cost eight "Gulden schweres Geld."

On the third of January, 1781, the English commander of Pensacola, Major General Campbell, ordered Colonel von Hanxleden, of the Waldeckers, to proceed with one hundred men of the 60th regiment, eleven mounted Provincials, 300 Indians, and 60 men of his own regiment, to the "French village on the Mississippi" to drive the Spaniards out of their intrenchments. On this occasion the Waldeck troops consisted of Captain von Baumbach, Lieutenants von Wilmowski and Stirling, ensign Ursal, six non-commissioned officers, two buglers, and forty-seven privates. Colonel von Hanxleden arrived in front of the enemy on the seventh of January, and attempted to take the Spanish works by assault. The Spaniards resisted stubbornly, and although the Germans repeatedly attacked with their bayonets, their courage was in vain, as their force was too small and as the Indians could not support them effectively. Colonel von Hanxleden died a hero's death leading his men, Lieutenant Stirling and the English Lieutenant Gordon fell, Captain von Baumbach and an officer of the provincials were wounded, and so were many others. The Spaniards, too, lost heavily, and one of their magazines was set on fire. The body of Colonel von Hanxleden was hastily buried under a large tree, and the Spaniards are said to have honored the dead hero by putting a fence around his grave.

The location of this battlefield is in doubt. The designation

"French village on the Mississippi" cannot be correct, for it would have taken Colonel von Hanxleden a great deal more than four days to reach the Mississippi from Pensacola, and his brave soldiers could not have returned to Pensacola on the ninth of January, two days after the fight. It must have been some French village between Pensacola and Mobile, and Mr. Hamilton, the author of "Colonial Mobile," a native Mobilian and a most painstaking and reliable authority, says: "This was on the coast below where the Apalache or Tensaw River empties into Mobile Bay."

After the fall of Mobile, Galvez went to Havana to secure reinforcements, and when these had arrived he appeared before Pensacola on the ninth of March, 1781, and two days later began the bombardment. This was continued, with some interruptions, for two months, when one of the powder magazines in the fort exploded, causing such devastation that the Spaniards were able to enter the fort in such numbers that further resistance was impossible. Then Pensacola surrendered on the ninth of May upon the same conditions as Baton Rouge had done. The prisoners were sent to New York. In Pensacola 800 men fought against 14,000, and Governor Galvez is said to have been greatly mortified when he heard that so small a number had resisted him for such a length of time. (See *Die deutschen Huelfstruppen im Nordamerik, Befreiungskrieg,"* by Max von Eelking, Hannover, 1883.)

In Pensacola the German troops, to their great surprise, found a countryman among the Indian chiefs. His name was "Brandenstein," and he had deserted as a soldier from Waldeck. After a very eventful career, he had become a fullfledged Indian, and even a chief. He served as an interpreter between the Germans and his tribe.

INDEX

d'Auvergne, Vicomte 14
Deubreuil 70, 94
Deucher 71
de Ulloa, Antonio, Governor 42, 43, 44, 45
de Vaca, Gabeza 2
de Vaudreuil, Pierre Francois de Rigaud Cavagnal, Marquis 60, 61
de Vaugine family 117
de Viceloque, Christine 97
de Villere family 117
    Joseph Rouer 43, 45, 46, 118
d'Iberville, Pierre le Moyne, Sieur 6
Dickson, Lieutenant Colonel 133, 134
Diehl, Caspar 82
    family 52, 54
Dire 95
Diron, M. 66, 73
Distelzweig, Anton 88
Dizier 95
d'Olhond family 117
Draeger family (Traeger) 122
Draeguer family (Traeger) 122
Draigue family (Traeger) 122
Dreiker family (Traeger) 122
Dreux, Mathurin 67
    Pierre 67
Droezler family (Troxler) 124
Drotseler family (Troxler) 124
Drotzeler family (Troxler) 124
Drozeler family (Troxler) 124
Dubs, Caspar 31, 77, 82, 83, 95, 103
    family 103, 124
    Louis 103
Ducros 95
Duffosat family 101
Dufresne, Dudemaine 37, 37 ftn., 75 ftn.
Duhaut 5
Dumanoir, Faucon 71, 72, 73
Dumont de Montigny 20, 23
Duparc 67
Dupratz 9, 25, 25 ftn.
Dupre family 101
Dupuy, Amilcar 108
    family 101

Dupuy, Felicie 108
Durel family 117
du Terrage, Marc Villiers 21 ftn.
Duvergé 20
Duvergier 66
Duverjé family 117

Eaufman family (Hofmann) 123, 125
Eckel, Jacob 103
Edeler family (Ettler) 122
Edelmeier family 123
    Johann Adam 89, 104
    Maria Barbara 89
    Marie Christine 89
Edler family (Ettler) 122
Edtl family (Ettler) 122
Eelking, Max von 136
Eldemere family (Edelmeier) 123
Elder, Elene 109
Elfer family (Helfer) 123
Elfert family (Helfer) 123
Elfre family (Helfer) 123
Elias, Mr. (Elias Stultheus) 21
Engel family 123
    Peter 93
Engelhardt family 123
    Philipp Jacob 111
Engle family (Engel) 123
    Peter 93
Estaidre family (Steiger) 124
Estilet family (Steilleder) 124
Estrenfoul family (Struempfl) 124
Etdell family (Heidel) 122
Etdelle family (Heidel) 123
Etlair family (Ettler) 122
Ettler, Agnes 122
    family 122, 124
    Johann 122
    Johannes 89, 102

Falteman family (Fellmann) 111
Faulse family (Foltz) 122
Fauquel family (Vogel) 123
Feaugle family (Vogel) 123
Febore family (Weber) 121
Febre family (Weber) 121
Fellmann family 111
    Joseph 111

Ory, Nikolaus (III) 111
   Pierre (I) 110
   Pierre (II) 110
Oser family (Hauser) 123
Oubre family (Huber) 93
   Jacob 104
   Jean George 31
Oufnague family (Hufnagel) 123
Oumas Indians 7, 75 ftn.
Ouuere family (Huber) 122
Ouvre family (Huber) 93, 122
   Jacob 104
   Jean George 31
Oxnard family 101
Oxtiger family (Achtziger) 125
Oxtixer family (Achtziger) 125

Pamonscaurse, Hour 124
Pascagoula Indians 22
Pauger, Adrien de 37
Paul, August 85
Pellerin, Henry 95
Pelloin 95
Pénicaut, André 19, 21, 22, 50
Percle family (Buerckel) 121
Percler family (Buerckel) 121
Perret, Amélie 64
   family 117
Perrinne, Torotay 124
Petit de Livilliers 95
Phelps, Albert 21
Philip, Father 63
Philippson, Christian 93
Pickett, Albert James 35
Picollier 95
Picou, Marie 110
Pictot, William 88
Pier, Juan Petit 111
Pineda 1, 2
Piquéry 95
Pircle family (Buerckel) 121
Pircli family (Buerckel) 121
Piseros family 101
   Miss 101
Poché, Felix Pierre, Chief Justice 113, 115
   Jacques 89
Poff, Daniel 93, 104

Poff, Renée 93
Pointe, Joseph Simon de la, Commodore 26
   Marie Simon de la 26, 27
Pollock family 116
Poltz family (Foltz) 122
Pommier 95
Porthier family 101
Poupart, Edward 80
Pujeau 95

Quaitret family (Ketterer) 124
Quarante, Mlle. 125
Quarantine, Mlle. (alias Hocman) 125
Quatrevingt family (Achtziger) 125
   Madame 125
Quellar family (Keller) 124
Queller family (Keller) 124
Querjac, Wilhelm (Ziriac) 81
Querne family (Kerner) 121
Quernel family (Kerner) 121, 123
Quimel family (Himmel) 123
Quinderman family (Kindermann) 121
Quindler family (Kindler) 121
Quindreman family (Kindermann) 121
Quinler family (Kindler) 121
Quisingre family (Kissinger) 124

Rabel, Jacob 104
Raeser, Anna Maria 65
   family 65
   Georg 104
   Johann Georg 84
Raffland, Daniel 102
Rapp, George 103
Raquet, M. 72
Rathbone family 117
Rauch, Bernhard 102
   Lorenz 102
Reggio, de, family 117
Rein, Joseph 109
Reine, Joseph 109
Reinhard, Margarethe 85
Remondet, Denis 110
Renner family 124